MY AIRSHIPS

MY AIRSHIPS

The Story of My Life
by

ALBERTO SANTOS-DUMONT

With a new Introduction by

AIR MARSHAL SIR PETER WYKEHAM
Deputy Chief of Air Staff, Royal Air Force

(author of *Santos-Dumont: A Study in Obsession*)

DOVER PUBLICATIONS, INC.
NEW YORK

This Dover edition, first published in 1973, is an unabridged republication of the English translation originally published in 1904 by Grant Richards, London, and The Century Company, New York. The work was first published in French in 1904 by Charpentier and Fasquelle, Paris, under the title *Dans l'air*.

A new introduction has been written especially for the present edition by Sir Peter Wykeham. This edition contains a new selection of pictures.

International Standard Book Number: 0-486-22122-9
Library of Congress Catalog Card Number: 71-145992

Manufactured in the United States of America
Dover Publications, Inc.
180 Varick Street
New York, N.Y. 10014

INTRODUCTION TO THE
DOVER EDITION

Do you love picking meat; or would you see
A man i' the clouds, and have him speak with thee?
                                                    BUNYAN

Alberto Santos-Dumont was the first man in Europe to fly an
aeroplane, within the accepted definition of the feat, and the next
in the world to do so after the Wrights. This alone should give him
a large enough place in history. But before he ever reached that
point he was already world-famous, to a degree hard to believe
sixty-five years later. In his day he was more famous, and famous
for longer, than the early astronauts. For public adulation perhaps
only Lindbergh, in the late twenties, rivals him in the field of aviation.

It is therefore strange to find him now, too often, among those
figures whom people recall without quite remembering anything
more than their name. Nobody needs reminding about Wilbur and
Orville Wright, and few are vague about Blériot, Farman, Count
Zeppelin. Santos-Dumont now, let me see — was he a balloonist?

He was indeed, and many other things besides. Because he has
been so badly treated by history, if for no other reason, I welcome
the reappearance of *My Airships*. But it is not necessary to es-
pouse his cause in order to enjoy his book. It is a delight in itself,
with its evocation of the age in which he lived, the background to
his most important years; and it is quite unnecessary for the reader,
whilst savouring its pages, to care for or to understand the progress
of early aviation. At the height of his first triumphs, immediately
after his thirtieth birthday, he dashed down onto paper a brilliant
portrait of the times, a picture of colour and light, much as the lately
established French school of painters had startled the world with

their new vision of Impressionism. And just as a great impulsive portrait tells more of a man than many pages of facts, so this book shows us more of his unique character than could possibly appear in the record, or for that matter in an introduction.

However, my own system is to read an introduction, if at all, *after* reading the book, and then one needs some facts. Alberto was sparing of these details, and one reason for his eclipse in history is his later reticence, almost secrecy, about his personal affairs. The book takes us only to the middle of his life, and leaves many questions unanswered. It is worth trying to fill in the portrait.

Alberto Santos-Dumont was born on the 20th July, 1873, his father's forty-first birthday, at Cabangu, in the João Aires district of Brazil. He was the seventh and youngest child of his parents, Henriques and Francisca Santos Dumont (characteristically, he himself added the hyphen to his surname). His father, who descended from a French immigrant family of skilled jewelsmiths, started life as an engineer, bought land, and eventually amassed a large fortune as a coffee planter. His mother, a woman of powerful and pious character, came of ancient Portuguese stock whose forebear had sailed into Rio with Dom João of Portugal when Napoleon drove him from his homeland in 1808. By descent, therefore, he was part aristocrat and part artisan.

Alberto spent his early years on his father's plantation, and soon showed himself fascinated by anything mechanical. In his youth, he was remarked to be brave, quick-witted, practical; and yet dreamy and introspective, and very much odd man out of his family, with their wealthy and stolid background. He received some technical education locally, together with his more conventional schooling, and read all the novels of Jules Verne at an early age.

Before he was seventeen years old the first turning point in his life arrived, when his father suffered a stroke and decided to sell his estates and move to Paris, where he could get the best medical attention. For the rest of the family this visit was a wonderful but temporary holiday. For Alberto it was almost a homecoming. Paris spoke to him, intrigued and entranced him, challenged him. It was love at first sight. Fervently he embraced the city; for the few months when he had to be away he pined for it, and as soon as he could he made it his physical as well as his mental home. There might be and were good enough reasons for this passion, for any boy from the Brazilian backwoods. The impact was overwhelming. But his reasons were perhaps a little surprising, and certainly were not the first which would leap to mind.

It is difficult to overemphasise the splendour of Paris in 1890, at the height of *la belle époque.* The whole artistic world looked towards her, and the gaiety and style of her society made other capitals seem drab by comparison; but the sciences, and engineering also, contributed to the brilliant glitter of her eminence, and provoked the envy of others. The city was filled with pioneers of every aspect of civilised life. She held some magic of inspiration which shone its light towards the frontiers of contemporary knowledge. It was a short period but glorious, and it coincided almost exactly with Alberto's dazzling career.

For though a poet at heart, his qualities and talents were all practical. It was the practical qualities of Paris which captured him. Avant-garde science and engineering, which had just demonstrated their prowess with the building of the Eiffel Tower, were there for his inspection. Alternative and more normal preoccupations for a rich young man, exemplified by the Moulin Rouge, by the Tabarin, by the world of Henri de Toulouse-Lautrec, concerned him not at all. He was a most unusual young Latin. No interest in women, or indeed any other sensual activities, ever diverted him from the great dream of his life. This dream was simply that man should learn to fly, and so, as in the lost dream of Daedalus, rise from his humble station to join the gods.

Few who met him could have detected this vision burning in the young student. Even his father did not suspect it. On Alberto's eighteenth birthday Henriques, feeling his end near, made over to him a full share of the coffee fortune; the father died shortly afterwards. The rest of the family went back to Brazil: Alberto remained. He organised the rest of his own education, and started on the pursuit of his dream.

His own words tell it best, if with restraint, but some of his special qualities must be underlined. Apart from his complete devotion to his quest, apart also from the money which enabled him to follow it, he had several other natural advantages. He was well if rather sketchily educated, particularly in scientific subjects, and had a devouring curiosity about almost anything. He spared no time for girls, and the minimum for polite society. He was brave, and also imaginative. He was small: short, nimble, and very light. He might himself have been designed for aviation, and his designs reflected his own characteristics.

These were very complex. He was foppish, vain, negligent in giving credit to others, and had that combined love and fear of celebrity which seems more appropriate to an entertainer than an inventor. He had an excellent opinion of himself. Above all, as with the city he lived in, he had *style*. His hats and gloves, the glimpse of the mother-of-pearl silk lining of his opera cloak, his high-lift shoes ("elevators"), his abnormally high collars (which became fashionable by the name of "Santos-Dumonts") and large shirt-cuffs, his beautifully prepared golden airships, his electric brougham, his striped-canvas hangars, his house off the Champs-Elysées: the whole picture of an "aerial sportsman" was a faultless creation, much of it studied, but even more of it an unconscious product of his character and his world.

It is all here, in his own book, written at the height of his first phase of fame and glory. When the story ends he is a world-famous figure, making the rounds of the principal capitals to receive the plaudits which were his just due. To our own age the whole business may seem overplayed. There is a temptation to ask what all the fuss was about, when such acclaim could be given to a man who manages to stagger seven miles, in still air, at less than a thousand feet, and later makes some highly uncertain trips around the out-skirts of Paris, punctuated by mishaps perilously close to slapstick comedy. His materials were simple enough; his designs incorpor-ated no new principles, and hardly any scientific discoveries beyond the internal combustion engine. Was he just a stunt man?

The answer is that the impact of his feats was not exaggerated, at the period when he did them, because with his airships he was the first man to succeed, not once but time after time, in leaving the ground, flying through the air to a place of his own choosing, and landing safely. In doing this he managed at last what the whole human race had dreamed of doing, since the remotest dawn of man's history. He did what so many had attempted and failed, with results farcical or tragic. What was more, he did it almost unaided. The first man in space was "placed in orbit" by a gigantic national effort. To the world of 1904, Santos-Dumont conquered the air single-handed. No wonder he was idolised.

At the end of *My Airships* he is looking towards the future, pro-phesying more and better lighter-than-air travel, mixing his engineering predictions with a curious flavour of fantasy which certainly owes a great deal to Jules Verne. He was an "aerial sportsman." He was a "professor of aerostation." But not for much longer. No sooner had the book gone to print than he began to hear rumours of the Wright Brothers.

The reticence of these great men concerning their early achievements is a fascinating aspect of their engaging characters, as different from Santos as it is possible to be, and it forms a surprising and interesting sideline on the history of early aviation. The news of their *Flyer* seeped through to Paris, though nobody really believed it, but it worried Santos sufficiently to make him revise all his ideas, and to take heavier-than-air flight seriously. He retreated from the public gaze, shut himself in his workshops, and set out to design and build an aeroplane.

In 1906 he emerged, bringing with him a powered canard box-kite, of frightening aspect, so designed as to be inherently unstable, and indeed probably uncontrollable by anyone other than a Santos-Dumont. After a series of pre-flight trials which included towing it along a high-wire by donkey-power, and attempting to fly it attached to one of his airships, he was ready for his attempt. By the time he lined it up in the Bois de Boulogne, in September 1906, the Wrights had already flown many hours at Dayton, and yet no credible report had reached Paris. Santos thought he was out in front.

After the delays, disappointments, even minor crack-ups, normally associated with inventors, he got his machine off the ground, on 23rd October, and flew for sixty metres. In November he did better, 220 metres, and so won the Archdeacon Prize for the first known (that is, fully known and accepted) heavier-than-air flight. Once again all Europe exploded with enthusiasm. Even the United States rang with his praise, for in scepticism of the Wright Brothers' achievements the U.S.A. seemed determined to lead the world.

This was the climax of his life. For another four years he stayed in the vanguard of aviation, though within a year there were others in the air: Farman, Voisin, Blériot, and several more. In particular the Wrights came out of the casual semi-obscurity of their early years, and in 1908 staggered Europe with their progress and their prowess, proving beyond doubt their claims to have been flying since 1903. Santos, designing and building his next aircraft, the

Demoiselle, was forced to swallow the bitter disappointment of slowly realising that he had not been the first. It was almost a unique position for an inventor so much in the public eye, but he took it well. He persisted with the *Demoiselle* (Dragonfly), refined it into a safe, practical, and simple light aircraft, and for another two years pursued his way as the "aerial sportsman," buzzing and hovering around the sunlit fields of France, the parks of Paris, the great houses of his wealthy friends.

In 1910 came tragedy. He had been feeling unwell. He visited his doctor, and after long consideration was told that he had disseminated sclerosis. No more fearful sentence could be pronounced. The disease was incurable, and would kill him in twenty years. In the meantime he could expect gradual reduction of his faculties, with impeded vision, weakness, unsteadiness, and dizzy spells. It was the end of his flying and perhaps, considering his temperament, the end of his life. His fastidiousness forced him into swift retirement from the world. He sold his house, his hangars and workshops, his aircraft; dispersed his helpers. He left Paris and became a melancholy wanderer, with no proper home, nor wife or children to support him in his time of blackest despair.

It is best not to dwell on the long twilight of the last period of his life. Though he had ups and downs his physical condition mercilessly deteriorated. Sometimes he was well enough to travel, and to take some interest in the feats of others, sometimes he spent long months in clinics. Twenty years passed. Towards the end he seemed to find a kind of peace, retiring to a house he built in Brazil. But increasingly he bowed under a mental burden, caused by his disease, in which he blamed himself for all the sorrows and ills which the invention of the aeroplane had brought to man. Self-persecuted, he burnt all his papers and records.

In his last days he tried to break out of the horrors his imagination heaped on his own conscience — aerial war, air disasters and crashes, airborne death and destruction — and tried to return to his vision of man the human bird; of the gift of flight given to the individual, flight so simple that, almost released from the trappings of machined metal, he could soar into the sun. . . .

But at last the inevitable claimed him. At the height of the civil war of 1932 Brazilian aircraft flew over his house, and he heard them bombing their own countrymen. The thread snapped. At sunset on the 23rd of July, just after his fifty-ninth birthday, he took his own life. In any case he had not long to live.

* * * * * * * *

A strange life: a heroic and fantastic character. Why was he then so neglected? Ten years before he died he was already almost forgotten. I think there are a number of reasons, though even the sum of them do not warrant such oblivion. Firstly, his own secretiveness, vastly exaggerated during his last years, made him destroy all his records. His diary, his letters, his notebooks and calculations, all were burnt. He had no children to honour his memory and explain him to posterity. His countrymen, wildly proud of his achievements but disproportionately horrified by the rumours of his death, determined to see him as they wanted him to be, and built up an image which did much to obscure the real man. The whole of South America, until recent years, championed him against the Wrights as the first man to fly, and made other almost equally far-fetched claims for his inventiveness. Consequently he rarely figures with much credit in the serious histories.

In the face of the clamour of his most devoted supporters, the rest of the world fell silent. It is unjust, but not unnatural. Now that all sides can look at him in the light of history, and old controversies are laid to rest, we can see him as a pioneer and as a man. He may richly deserve the mantle of a national hero, but it does not fit him well enough to show him as he was. He was greater than that.

A Santos-Dumont aircraft was more than an invented apparatus — it was an artistic composition — a brave, bright, exquisite thing, beautifully fashioned in every detail. He spun his designs out of his own character, for he was exactly like them. Both he and they were often on the wrong track, victims of serious setbacks, suffering uncouth mishaps. But his courage, his style, his *panache,* at least as much as his science and skill, kept his delicate craft in the air: higher, farther, faster. The huge Parisian crowds held their breath. Seeing him fly was like watching an iridescent soap bubble floating in the sunlight, waiting for it to vanish, but hoping it would survive.

Perhaps it must be admitted that he made a comparatively small contribution to the great flowing-together of theoretical knowledge from many inventive brains, which added to the conquest of the air. He was not so good a designer as the Wrights, nor so good an engineer. But this is not enough to turn him into an obscure second-prize winner. He had something special of his own.

He was the great empiricist, one of the best examples in technical history of the man determined to "try it and find out." Most of his hair-raising experiences came from pushing this system to the limit. While others talked, sketched, deliberated, he acted. At the Great Parisian Exposition of 1900 a Congress of Aviation debated in the Grand Palais. When the leading professors of the day held forth on the subject of aviation, and debated whether man could fly, Santos was absent from the floor. He was overhead in his fourth airship.

His approach to his problems was practical and direct. His designs were simple and light. It was a doctrine with him. He took pleasure in showing what a man can do if he is skilful, brave, ingenious, and makes straight for his objective, unhampered by the doubts, fears, and compromises of others.

Half of his life is in this book, by far the happier half. Happy is he who loves his life's work, and his love and absorption rise up from every page. He does not find room here to describe two minor aspects of his activities which illustrate his dedication: the first, that he and his De Dion tricycle were hoisted into a tree in the Bois de Boulogne with the engine running to test the vibration of the structure when airborne; and the second, that he had a room in his house where the furniture was suspended close to the ceiling, so that he could get the feeling for eating in the basket of an airship. But he would not have minded setting down these facts, nor have thought them noteworthy or eccentric. He considered they were necessary, and that was all that mattered.

I do not mind admitting that for me, as perhaps for many others, much of the fascination of his work, and this his book about it, lies in a powerful self-identification. How one longs to be him, with his freedom and his opportunities! How strongly burns this longing in modern man, caught in the iron grip of organisation and society, pinioned by endless webs of regulations, numbed by committees, deadened by mass communications, baffled by restrictions, and frustrated by endless, nameless, faceless authorities.

How good to be in Paris, young, rich, intelligent, courageous, with the air still to be conquered! To be able to make all the decisions, rely on one's own skill, pick up all the checks, dazzle the *haut monde,* indulge a harmless taste for exhibitionism. To drift over the lovely countryside of France and hear the cocks crowing in the first hint of morning; to watch the sun come up and the mists dissolve, showing the fields and rivers lying in the haze of a new day. To feel the work of your own brain and hands bear you up and obey you. To live life as it may never be lived again, with grace and spirit and a careless exhilaration.

To fly in summer over the most beautiful city in the world, in a golden airship, trailing a scarlet banner behind!

PETER WYKEHAM

London
January 1973

CONTENTS

List of illustrations xvii
Introductory Fable
        The Reasoning of Children 1
  I. The Coffee Plantation 6
  II. Paris; Professional Balloonists, Automobiles 11
  III. My First Balloon Ascent 15
  IV. My "Brazil," Smallest of Spherical Balloons 20
  V. The Real and the Imaginary Dangers of Ballooning . 24
  VI. I Yield to the Steerable Balloon Idea 29
  VII. My First Airship Cruises (1898) 35
  VIII. How It Feels to Navigate the Air 39
  IX. Explosive Engines and Inflammable Gases 44
  X. I Go in for Airship Building 49
  XI. The Exposition Summer 54
  XII. The Deutsch Prize and Its Problems 60
  XIII. A Fall before a Rise 64
  XIV. The Building of My "No. 6" 69
  XV. Winning the Deutsch Prize 72
  XVI. A Glance Backward and Forward 76
  XVII. Monaco and the Maritime Guide Rope 79
  XVIII. Flights in Mediterranean Winds 85
  XIX. Speed 90
  XX. An Accident and Its Lessons 96
  XXI. The First of the World's Airship Stations 99
  XXII. My "No. 9," the Little Runabout 105
  XXIII. The Airship in War 111
  XXIV. Paris as a Center of Airship Experiments 117
Concluding Fable
        More Reasoning of Children 121

LIST OF ILLUSTRATIONS

on or facing page

Frontispiece

Alberto Santos-Dumont ii

1. Alberto Santos-Dumont winning the Deutsch Prize 4
2. Santos-Dumont's parents 5
3. Private railway on the Santos-Dumont coffee
   plantation 8
4. The Santos-Dumont coffee plantation in Brazil 9
5. My "Brazil," smallest of the spherical balloons 22
6. The rooftops of Paris 23
7. The "Santos-Dumont No. 1" 36
8. Motor of the "Santos-Dumont No. 1" 37
9. *Retour de flamme* over the Île de Puteaux 48
10. First start in the "Santos-Dumont No. 2" 49
11. Accident to the "Santos-Dumont No. 2,"
    May 11, 1899 (first phase) 50
12. Accident to the "Santos-Dumont No. 2,"
    May 11, 1899 (second phase) 51
13. Accident to the "Santos-Dumont No. 2,"
    May 11, 1899 (third phase) 52
14. The "Santos-Dumont No. 3" 53
15. Professor Langley visits the "Santos-Dumont No. 4" ... 56
16. Motor of the "Santos-Dumont No. 4" 57
17. The "Santos-Dumont No. 5" 62
18. The "Santos-Dumont No. 5" landing at the
    Trocadéro for repairs 63
19. The "Santos-Dumont No. 5" over the Longchamps
    racecourse 64
20. Accident in the park of M. Edmond Rothschild 65

21. Accident at the Trocadéro Hotel, just before
    rescue by firemen 68
22. The "Santos-Dumont No. 6" 69
23. Accident to the "Santos-Dumont No. 6" 70
24. Motor of the "Santos-Dumont No. 6" 71
25. The "Santos-Dumont No. 6" leaving the balloon
    shed at the Aéro Club, Saint Cloud 72
26. Rounding the Eiffel Tower on the way to winning
    the Deutsch Prize 73
27. Scientific commission of the Aéro Club observing
    the winning of the Deutsch Prize 74
28. Medal awarded to Santos-Dumont by the
    Brazilian government 75
29. In the Bay of Monaco 78
30. From Cap Martin to Monte Carlo 79
31. The balloon house at La Condamine 82
32. Interior of the balloon shed, Monte Carlo 83
33. Santos-Dumont being lifted over the sea wall 84
34. The "Santos-Dumont No. 7" 85
35. "Wind A" and "Wind B" 86
36. From the balloon house at La Condamine,
    February 12, 1902 87
37. Accident, February 14, 1902. Phases A and B 96
38. Accident, February 14, 1902. Phases C and D 97
39. Airship station, Neuilly St. James 100
40. "The Omnibus" 101
41. The "Santos-Dumont No. 9" over the Bois de
    Boulogne 106
42. Santos-Dumont lands at his own front door 107
43. The "Santos-Dumont No. 9," the little runabout 112
44. The "Santos-Dumont No. 9" at military review,
    July 14, 1903 113
45. Guide roping over the housetops 118
46. Guide roping lower than the housetops 119

MY AIRSHIPS

THE REASONING OF CHILDREN

Two young Brazilian boys strolled in the shade conversing. They were simple youths of the interior, knowing only the plenty of the primitive plantation, where, undisturbed by labor-saving devices, Nature yielded man her fruits at the price of the sweat of his brow.

They were ignorant of machines to the extent that they had never seen a wagon or a wheelbarrow. Horses and oxen bore the burdens of plantation life on their backs, and placid Indian laborers wielded the spade and the hoe.

Yet they were thoughtful boys. At this moment they discussed things beyond all that they had seen or heard.

"Why not devise a better means of transport than the backs of horses and of oxen?" Luis argued. "Last summer I hitched horses to a barn door, loaded it with sacks of maize, and hauled in one load what ten horses could not have brought on their backs. True, it required seven horses to drag it, while five men had to sit around its edges and hold the load from falling off."

"What would you have?" answered Pedro. "Nature demands compensations. You cannot get something from nothing or more from less!"

"If we could put rollers under the drag, less pulling power would be needed."

"Bah! the force saved would be used up in the labor of shifting the rollers."

"The rollers might be attached to the drag at fixed points by means of holes running through their centers," mused Luis. "Or why should not circular blocks of wood be fixed at the four corners of the drag? . . . Pedro! look down the road, what is coming?

The very thing I imagined, only better! One horse is pulling it at a good trot!"

The first wagon to appear in that region of the interior stopped, and its driver spoke with the boys.

"Those round things?" he answered to their questions; "they are called wheels."

Pedro accepted his explanation of the principle slowly.

"There must be some hidden defect in the device," he insisted. "Look around us. Nowhere does Nature employ the device you call the wheel. Observe the mechanism of the human body. Observe the horse's frame. Observe . . . "

"Observe that horse and man and wagon with its wheels are speeding from us," replied Luis, laughing. "Cannot you yield to accomplished facts? You tire me with your appeals to Nature. Has man ever accomplished anything worth having except by combating Nature? We do violence to her when we chop down a tree! I would go further than this invention of the wagon. Conceive a more powerful motive force than that horse . . . "

"Attach two horses to the wagon."

"I mean a machine," said Luis.

"A mechanical horse with powerful iron legs!" suggested Pedro.

"No; I would have a motor wagon. If I could find an artificial force, I would cause it to act on a point in the circumference of each wheel. Then the wagon could carry its own puller!"

"You might as well attempt to lift yourself from the ground by pulling at your bootstraps!" laughed Pedro. "Listen, Luis. Man is subject to certain natural laws. The horse, it is true, carries more than his own weight, but by a device of Nature's own — his legs. Had you the artificial force you dream of, you would have to apply it naturally. I have it! It would have to be applied to poles to push your wagon from behind!"

"I hold to applying the force to the wheels," insisted Luis.

"By the nature of things you would lose power," said Pedro. "A wheel is harder to force on from a point inside its circumference than when the motive power is applied to that circumference directly, as by pushing or pulling the wagon."

"To relieve friction I would run my power wagon on smooth iron rails. Then the loss in power would be gained in speed."

"Smooth iron rails!" laughed Pedro. "Why, the wheels would slip on them! You would have to put notches all round their circumference and corresponding notches in the rails. And what would prevent the power wagon slipping off the rails even then?"

The boys had been walking briskly. Now a shrieking noise startled them. Before them stretched in long lines a railway in course of construction and from among the hills came toward them, at what seemed immense speed, a construction train.

"It is an avalanche!" cried Pedro.

"It is the very thing that I was dreaming of!" said Luis.

The train stopped. A gang of laborers emerged from it and began working on the road-bed, while the locomotive engineer answered the boys' questions and explained the mechanism of his engine. The boys discussed this later wonder as they wended their way homeward.

"Could it be adapted to the river, men might become lords of the water as of the land," said Luis. "It would be necessary only to devise wheels capable of taking hold of the water. Fix them to a great frame, like that wagon body, and the steam engine could propel it along the surface of the river!"

"Now you talk folly!" exclaimed Pedro. "Does a fish float on the surface? In the water we must travel as the fish does — in it, not over it! Your wagon body, being filled with light air, would upset at your first movement. And your wheels — do you imagine they would take hold of so liquid a thing as water?"

"What would you suggest?"

"I would suggest that your water wagon be jointed in half a dozen places, so that it could be made to squirm through the water like a fish. Listen! A fish navigates the water. You desire to navigate the water. Then study the fish! There are fish that use propeller fins and flippers, too. So you might devise broad boards to strike the water as our hands and feet strike it in swimming. But do not talk about wagon wheels in the water!"

They were now beside the broad river. The first steamer to navigate it was seen approaching from a distance. The boys could not yet well distinguish it.

"It is evidently a whale," said Pedro. "What navigates the water? Fish. What is the fish that sometimes is seen swimming with its body halfway above the surface? The whale. See, it is spouting water!"

"That is not water, but steam or smoke," said Luis.

"Then it is a dead whale; and the steam is the vapor of putrefaction. That is why it stays so high in the water — a dead whale rises high, on its back."

"No," said Luis. "It is really a steam water wagon."

"With smoke coming from fire in it, as from the locomotive?"

"Yes."

"But the fire would burn it up. . . . "

"The body is doubtless iron, like the locomotive."

"Iron would sink. Throw your hatchet in the river and see."

The steamboat came to shore, close to the boys. Running to it, to their joy they perceived on its deck an old friend of their family, a neighboring planter.

"Come, boys!" he said; "and I will show you round this steamboat."

After a long inspection of the machinery, the two boys sat with their old friend on the fore-deck, in the shade of an awning.

"Pedro," said Luis, "will not men some day invent a ship to sail in the sky?"

The common-sense old planter glanced with apprehension at the youth's face, flushed with ardor.

"Have you been much in the sun, Luis?" he asked.

"Oh, he is always talking in that flighty way," Pedro reassured him. "He takes pleasure in it."

"No, my boy," said the planter. "Man will never navigate a ship in the sky."

"But on St. John's Eve, when we all make bonfires, we also send up little tissue-paper spheres with hot air in them," insisted Luis. "If we could construct a very great one, big enough to lift a man, a light car, and a motor, might not the whole system be propelled through the air as a steamboat is propelled through the water?"

"Boys, never talk foolishness!" exclaimed the old friend of the family, hurriedly, as the captain of the boat approached. It was too late. The captain had heard the boy's observation; instead of calling it folly, he excused him.

"The great balloon which you imagine has existed since 1783," he said. "But, though capable of carrying a man or several men, it cannot be controlled. It is at the mercy of the slightest breeze. As long ago as 1852, a French engineer named Giffard made a brilliant failure with what he called a 'dirigible balloon,' furnished with the motor and propeller Luis has dreamed of. All he did was to demonstrate the impossibility of directing a balloon through the air."

1. Alberto Santos-Dumont winning the Deutsch Prize

2.   Santos-Dumont's parents

"The only way would be to build a flying machine on the model of the bird," spoke up Pedro, with authority.

"Pedro is a very sensible boy," observed the old planter. "It is a pity Luis is not more like him and less visionary. Tell me, Pedro, how did you come to decide in favor of the bird as against the balloon?"

"Easily," replied Pedro, glibly. "It is the most ordinary common sense. Does man fly? No. Does the bird fly? Yes. Then, if man would fly, let him imitate the bird. Nature has made the bird; and Nature never goes wrong. Had the bird been furnished with a great air bag, I might have suggested a balloon. . . .

"Exactly!" exclaimed both captain and planter.

But Luis, sitting in his corner, muttered, unconvinced as Galileo: "It will move!"

CHAPTER I

THE COFFEE PLANTATION

From the way in which the partisans of Nature have fallen upon me, I might well be the uninformed and visionary Luis of the fable; for has it not been taken for granted that I began my experiments ignorant alike of mechanics and ballooning? And before my experiments succeeded were they not all called impossible?

Does not the final condemnation of the common-sense Pedro continue to weigh upon me?

After steering my ship through the sky at will, I am still told that flying creatures are heavier than the air. A little more, and I should be made responsible for the tragic accidents of others who had not my experience of mechanics and aeronautics.

On the whole, therefore, I think it best to begin at the coffee plantation where I was born in the year 1873.

Inhabitants of Europe comically picture these Brazilian plantations to themselves as primitive stations of the boundless pampas, as innocent of the cart and the wheelbarrow as of the electric light and the telephone. There are such stations far in the interior. I have been through them on hunting trips; but they are not the coffee plantations of São Paulo.

I can hardly imagine a more stimulating environment for a boy dreaming over mechanical inventions. At the age of seven I was permitted to drive our "locomobiles" of the epoch — steam traction-engines of the fields, with great broad wheels. At the age of twelve I had conquered my place in the cabs of the Baldwin locomotive engines, hauling trainloads of green coffee over the sixty miles of our plantation railway. When my father and brothers would take pleasure in making horseback trips far and near, to see if the trees were clean, if the crops were coming up, and if the rains had done damage, I preferred to slip down to the Works and play with the coffee-engines.

I think it is not generally understood how scientifically a Brazilian coffee plantation may be operated. From the moment when a railway train has brought the green berries to the Works to the moment when the finished and assorted product is loaded on the transatlantic ships, no human hand touches the coffee.

You know that the berries of black coffee are red when they are green. Though it may complicate the statement, they look like cherries. Carloads of them are unloaded at the central works and thrown into great tanks, where the water is continually renewed and agitated. Mud that has clung to the berries from the rains, and little stones which have become mixed with them in the loading of the cars, go to the bottom, while the berries and the little sticks and bits of leaves float on the surface and are carried from the tank by means of an inclined trough, whose bottom is pierced with innumerable little holes. Through these holes falls some of the water with the berries, while the little sticks and pieces of leaves float on.

The fallen coffee berries are now clean. They are still the color and size of cherries. The red exterior is a hard pod, or *polpa.* Inside of each pod are two beans, each of which is covered with a skin of its own. The water which has fallen with the berries carries them on to the machine called the *despolpador,* which breaks the outside pod and frees the beans. Long tubes, called "driers," now receive the beans, still wet and with their skins still on them. In these driers the beans are continually agitated in hot air.

Coffee is very delicate. It must be handled carefully. Therefore the dried beans are lifted by the cups of an endless-chain elevator to a height whence they slide down an inclined trough to another building because of the danger of fire. This is the coffee machine house.

The first machine is a ventilator in which sieves shaken back and forth are so combined that only the coffee beans can pass through them. No coffee is lost in them, and no dirt is kept by them; for one little stone or stick that may still have been carried with the beans would be enough to break the next machine.

Another endless-chain elevator carries the beans to a height whence they fall through an inclined trough into the *descascador,* or "skinner." It is a highly delicate machine; if the spaces between are a trifle too big, the coffee passes without being skinned, while if they are too small, they break the beans.

Another elevator carries the skinned beans with their skins to another ventilator, in which the skins are blown away.

Still another elevator takes the now clean beans up and throws them into the "separator," a great copper tube two yards in diameter and about seven yards long, resting at a slight incline. Through the separator tube the coffee slides. As it is pierced at first with little holes, the smaller beans fall through them. Further along it is pierced with larger holes, and through these the medium-sized beans fall; and further still along are yet larger holes for the large, round beans called "mocha."

The machine is called a separator because it separates the beans into their conventional grades by size. Each grade falls into its hopper, beneath which are stationed weighing scales and men with coffee sacks. As the sacks fill up to the required weight, they are replaced by empty ones; and the tied and labeled sacks are shipped to Europe.

As a boy, I played with this machinery and the driving engines that furnished its motive force; and before long familiarity had taught me how to repair any part of it. As I have said, it is delicate machinery. In particular, the moving sieves were continually getting out of order. While they were not heavy, they moved back and forth horizontally at great speed and took an enormous amount of motive power. The belts were always being changed, and I remember the fruitless efforts of all of us to remedy the mechanical defects of the device.

Now, is it not curious that these troublesome shifting sieves were the only machines at the coffee works that were not rotary? They were not rotary, and they were bad. I think this put me, as a boy, against all *agitating* devices in mechanics, and in favor of the more easily handled and more serviceable rotary movement.

It may be that half a century from now man will assume mastery of the air by means of flying machines heavier than the medium in which they move. I look forward to the time with hope; and at the present moment I have gone further to meet it than any other, because my own airships (which have been so reproached on this head) are slightly heavier than the air. But I am prejudiced enough to think that, when the time comes, the conquering device will not be flapping wings or any other substitute of an agitating nature.

3. Private railway on the Santos-Dumont coffee plantation

4. The Santos-Dumont coffee plantation in Brazil

I cannot say at what age I made my first kites, but I remember how my comrades used to tease me at our game of "Pigeon flies!" All the children gather round a table and the leader calls out: "Pigeon flies! Hen flies! Crow flies! Bee flies!" and so on; and at each call we were supposed to raise our fingers. Sometimes, however, he would call out: "Dog flies! Fox flies!" or some other like impossibility, to catch us. If anyone raised a finger, he was made to pay a forfeit. Now my playmates never failed to wink and smile mockingly at me when one of them called: "Man flies!" for at the word I would always lift my finger very high, as a sign of absolute conviction; and I refused with energy to pay the forfeit. The more they laughed at me, the happier I was, hoping that someday the laugh would be on my side.

Among the thousands of letters which I received after winning the Deutsch Prize, there was one that gave me particular pleasure. I quote from it as a matter of curiosity:

> ...Do you remember the time, my dear Alberto, when we played together "Pigeon flies!"? It came back to me suddenly the day when the news of your success reached Rio.
>
> "Man flies!" old fellow! You were right to raise your finger, and you have just proved it by flying round the Eiffel Tower.
>
> You were right not to pay the forfeit; it is M. Deutsch who has paid it in your stead. Bravo! you well deserve the 100,000 franc prize.
>
> They play the old game now more than ever at home; but the name has been changed and the rules modified since October 19, 1901. They call it now "Man flies!" and he who does not raise his finger at the word pays his forfeit.
>
> Your friend,
> PEDRO

This letter brings back to me the happiest days of my life, when I amused myself, while waiting for something better, in making light aeroplanes with bits of straw, moved by screw propellers driven by springs of twisted rubber, or ephemeral silk-paper balloons. Each year, on June 24, over the St. John bonfires which are customary in Brazil from long tradition, I inflated whole fleets of these little Montgolfiers and watched in ecstasy their ascension to the skies.

In those days, I confess, my favorite author was Jules Verne. The wholesome imagination of this truly great writer, working magically with the immutable laws of matter, fascinated me from childhood.

In its daring conceptions I saw, never doubting, the mechanics and the science of the coming ages, when man should, by his unaided genius, rise to the height of a demigod.

With Captain Nemo and his shipwrecked guests I explored the depths of the sea in that first of all submarines, the *Nautilus.* With Phineas Fogg I went round the world in eighty days. In *Screw Island* and *The Steam House* my boyish faith leaped out to welcome the ultimate triumphs of an automobilism that, in those days, had not as yet a name. With Hector Servadoc I navigated the air!

I saw my first balloon in 1888, when I was about fifteen years old. There was a fair or celebration of some sort at the town of São Paulo, and a professional made the ascent, letting himself down afterward in a parachute. By this time I was perfectly familiar with the history of Montgolfier and the balloon craze which, following on his courageous and brilliant experiments, so significantly marked the last years of the eighteenth and the first years of the nineteenth century. In my heart I had the deepest admiration for those four men of genius — Montgolfier and the physicists Charles and Pilâtre de Rozier, and the engineer Henri Giffard — who have attached their names forever to great steps forward in aerial navigation.

I, too, desired to go ballooning. In the long, sun-bathed Brazilian afternoons, when the hum of insects, punctuated by the far-off cry of some bird, lulled me, I would lie in the shade of the veranda and gaze into the fair sky of Brazil, where the birds fly so high and soar with such ease on their great outstretched wings, where the clouds mount so gaily in the pure light of day, and you have only to raise your eyes to fall in love with space and freedom. So, musing on the exploration of the aerial ocean, I, too, devised airships and flying machines in my imagination.

These imaginings I kept to myself. In those days, in Brazil, to talk of inventing a flying machine, or dirigible balloon, would have been to stamp one's self as unbalanced and visionary. Spherical balloonists were looked on as daring professionals not differing greatly from acrobats; and for the son of a planter to dream of emulating them would have been almost a social sin.

CHAPTER II

PARIS; PROFESSIONAL BALLOONISTS, AUTOMOBILES

In 1891 it was decided that our family should make a trip to Paris, and I rejoiced doubly at the prospect. All good Americans are said to go to Paris when they die. But to me, with the bias of my reading, France — the land of my father's ancestors and of his own education as an engineer at the École Centrale — represented everything that is powerful and progressive.

In France the first hydrogen balloon had been let loose and the first airship had been made to navigate the air with its steam engine, screw propeller, and rudder. Naturally, I figured to myself that the problem had made marked progress since Henri Giffard in 1852, with a courage equal to his science, gave his masterly demonstration of the problem of directing balloons.

I said to myself, "I am going to Paris to see the new things — steerable balloons and automobiles!"

On one of my first free afternoons, therefore, I slipped away from the family on a tour of exploration. To my immense astonishment, I learned that there were no steerable balloons — that there were only spherical balloons, like that of Charles in 1783! In fact, no one had continued the trials of an elongated balloon driven by a thermic motor, begun by Henri Giffard. The trials of such balloons with an electric motor, undertaken by the Tissandier brothers in 1883, had been repeated by two constructors in the following year, but had been finally given up in 1885. For years no "cigar-shaped" balloon had been seen in the air.

This threw me back on spherical ballooning. Consulting the Paris city directory, I noted the address of a professional aeronaut. To him I explained my desires.

"You want to make an ascent?" he asked gravely. "Hum, hum! Are you sure you have the courage? A balloon ascent is no small thing, and you seem too young."

I assured him both of my purpose and my courage. Finally he yielded to my arguments, and consented to take me "for a short ascent." It must be on a calm, sunny afternoon, and not last more than two hours.

"My honorarium will be 1200 francs," he added; "and you must sign me a contract to hold yourself responsible for all damage we may do to your own life and limbs, and to mine, to the property of third parties, and to the balloon itself and its accessories. Furthermore, you agree to pay our railway fares and transportation for the balloon and its basket back to Paris from the point at which we come to the ground."

I asked time for reflection. To a youth eighteen years of age, 1200 francs was a large sum. How could I justify the spending of it to my parents? Then I reflected:

"If I risk 1200 francs for an afternoon's pleasure, I shall find it either good or bad. If it is bad, the money will be lost. If it is good, I shall want to repeat it and I shall not have the means."

This decided me. Regretfully, I gave up ballooning and took refuge in automobiling.

Automobiles were still rare in Paris in 1891, and I had to go to the works at Valentigny to buy my first machine, a Peugeot 3½ horsepower roadster.

It was a curiosity. In those days there were no automobile licenses, no "chauffeurs'" examinations. We drove our new inventions through the streets of the capital at our own risks and perils. Such was the curiosity they aroused that I was not allowed to stop in public places like the Place de l'Opéra for fear of attracting multitudes and obstructing traffic.

Immediately I became an enthusiastic automobilist. I took pleasure in understanding the parts and their proper interworking; I learned to care for my machine and to repair it; and when, at the end of some seven months, our whole family returned to Brazil, I took the Peugeot roadster with me.

Returning to Paris in 1892, with the balloon idea still obsessing me, I looked up a number of other professional aeronauts. Like the first, all wanted extravagant sums to take me up with them on the most trivial kind of ascent. All took the same attitude. They made a danger and a difficulty of ballooning, enlarging on its risks to life and property. Even in presence of the great prices they proposed to charge me, they did not encourage me to close with them. Obviously they were determined to keep ballooning to themselves as a professional mystery. Therefore, I bought a new automobile.

I should add that this condition of things has changed wonderfully since the foundation of the Paris Aéro Club.

Automobile tricycles were just then coming to the fore. I chose one and rejoiced in its freedom from breakdowns. In my new enthusiasm for the type, I was the first to introduce motor-tricycle races in Paris. Renting the bicycle track of the Parc des Princes for an afternoon, I organized the race and offered the prizes. "Common-sense" people declared that the event would end disastrously; they proved to their own satisfaction that the tricycles, going round the short curves of a bicycle track, would overturn and wreck themselves. If they did not do this, the inclination would certainly cause the carburetor to stop or not to work so well; and the stoppage of the carburetor while going around a sharp curve would upset the tricycles. The director of the Vélodrome, while accepting my money, refused to let me have the track for a Sunday afternoon, fearing a fiasco! They were disappointed when the race proved to be a great success.

Returning again to Brazil, I regretted bitterly that I had not persevered in my attempt to make a balloon ascent. At that distance, far from ballooning possibilities, even the high prices demanded by the aeronauts seemed to me of secondary importance. Finally, one day in 1897, in a Rio bookshop, when making my purchases of reading matter for a new voyage to Paris, I came on a volume by MM. Lachambre and Machuron — *Andrée: Au Pôle Nord en Ballon.*

The reading of this book during the long sea voyage proved a revelation to me, and I finished by studying it like a textbook. Its description of materials and prices opened my eyes. At last I saw clearly. Andrée's immense balloon — a reproduction of whose photograph on the book cover showed how those who gave it the final varnishing climbed up its sides and over its summit like a mountain — cost only 40,000 francs to construct and equip fully!

I determined that, on arriving in Paris, I would cease consulting professional aeronauts and would make the acquaintance of constructors.

I was particularly anxious to meet M. Lachambre, the builder of the Andrée balloon, and M. Machuron, who was his associate and the writer of the book. In these men I will say frankly that I found all I had hoped for. When I asked M. Lachambre how much it would cost me to take a short trip in one of his balloons, his reply so astonished me that I asked him to repeat it.

"For a long trip of three or four hours," he said, "it will cost you 250 francs, all expenses and return of balloon by rail included."

"And the damages?" I asked.

"We shall not do any damage!" he replied, laughing.

I closed with him on the spot, and M. Machuron agreed to take me up the next day.

CHAPTER III

MY FIRST BALLOON ASCENT

I have kept the clearest remembrance of the delightful sensations I experienced in this day, my first trial in the air. I arrived early at the Parc d'Aérostation of Vaugirard, so as to lose nothing of the preparation.

The balloon, of a capacity of 750 cubic meters (26,500 cubic feet), was lying a flat mass on the grass. At a signal from M. Lachambre, the workmen turned on the gas, and soon the formless thing rounded up into a great sphere and rose into the air.

At 11 A.M. all was ready. The basket rocked prettily beneath the balloon, which a mild, fresh breeze was caressing. Impatient to be off, I stood in my corner of the narrow wicker basket, with a bag of ballast in my hand. In the other corner M. Machuron gave the word: "Let go, all!"

Suddenly the wind ceased. The air seemed motionless around us. We were off, going at the speed of the air current in which we now lived and moved. Indeed, for us there was no more wind; and this is the first great fact of all spherical ballooning. Infinitely gentle is this unfelt movement forward and upward. The illusion is complete: it seems not to be the balloon that moves, but the earth that sinks down and away.

At the bottom of the abyss which already opened 1500 yards below us, the earth, instead of appearing round like a ball, shows concave like a bowl by a peculiar phenomenon of refraction whose effect is to lift up constantly to the aeronaut's eyes the circle of the horizon.

Villages and woods, meadows and châteaux, pass across the moving scene, out of which the whistling of locomotives throws sharp notes. These faint, piercing sounds, together with the yelping and barking of dogs, are the only noises that reach one through the depths of the upper air. The human voice cannot mount up into these boundless solitudes. Human beings look like ants along the white lines that are highways, and the rows of houses look like children's playthings.

While my gaze was still held fascinated on the scene, a cloud passed before the sun. Its shadow cooled the gas in the balloon, which wrinkled and began descending, gently at first and then with accelerated speed, against which we strove by throwing out ballast. This is the second great fact of spherical ballooning — we are masters of our altitude by the possession of a few pounds of sand!

Regaining our equilibrium above a plateau of clouds at about 3000 yards, we enjoyed a wonderful sight. The sun cast the shadow of the balloon on this screen of dazzling whiteness, while our own profiles, magnified to giant size, appeared in the center of a triple rainbow! As we could no longer see the earth, all sensation of movement ceased. We might be going at storm speed and not know it. We could not even know the direction we were taking, save by descending below the clouds to regain our bearings!

A joyous peal of bells mounted up to us. It was the noonday Angelus, ringing from some village belfry. I had brought up with us a substantial lunch of hard-boiled eggs, cold roast beef and chicken, cheese, ice cream, fruits and cakes, Champagne, coffee and Chartreuse. Nothing is more delicious than lunching like this above the clouds in a spherical balloon. No dining room can be so marvelous in its decoration. The sun sets the clouds in ebullition, making them throw up rainbow jets of frozen vapor like great sheaves of fireworks all around the table. Lovely white spangles of the most delicate ice formation scatter here and there by magic, while flakes of snow form moment by moment out of nothingness, beneath our very eyes, and in our very drinking glasses!

I was finishing my little glass of liqueur when the curtain suddenly fell on this wonderful stage setting of sunlight, cloud billows, and azure. The barometer rose rapidly five millimeters, showing an abrupt rupture of equilibrium and a swift descent. Probably the balloon had become loaded down with several pounds of snow, and it was falling into a cloud.

We passed into the half-darkness of the fog. We could still see our basket, our instruments, and the parts of the rigging nearest us, but the netting that held us to the balloon was visible only to a certain height and the balloon itself had completely disappeared. So we had for a moment the strange and delightful sensation of hanging in the void without support, of having lost our last ounce of weight in a limbo of nothingness, somber and portentous!

After a few minutes of fall, slackened by throwing out more ballast, we found ourselves under the clouds at a distance of about 300 yards from the ground. A village fled away from us below. We took our bearings with the compass and compared our route map with the immense natural map that unfolded below. Soon we could identify roads, railways, villages, and forests, all hastening toward us from the horizon with the swiftness of the wind itself!

The storm which had sent us downward marked a change of weather. Now little gusts began to push the balloon from right to left, up and down. From time to time the guide rope — a great rope dangling 100 yards below our basket — would touch earth; and soon the basket, too, began to graze the tops of trees.

What is called "guide-roping" thus began for me under conditions peculiarly instructive. We had a sack of ballast at hand; and when some special obstacle rose in our path, like a tree or a house, we threw out a few handfuls of sand to leap up and pass over it. More than 50 yards of the guide rope dragged behind us on the ground; and this was more than enough to keep our equilibrium under the altitude of 100 yards above which we decided not to rise for the rest of the trip.

This first ascent allowed me to appreciate fully the utility of this simple part of the spherical balloon's rigging, without which its landing would usually present grave difficulties. When, for one reason or another — humidity gathering on the surface of the balloon, a downward stroke of wind, accidental loss of gas, or, more frequently, the passing of a cloud before the face of the sun — the balloon came back to earth with disquieting speed, the guide rope would come to rest in part on the ground, and so, unballasting the whole system by so much of its weight, stopped, or at least eased, the fall. Under contrary conditions, any too rapid upward tendency of the balloon was counterbalanced by the lifting of the guide rope off the ground, so that a little more of its weight became added to the weight of the floating system of the moment before.

Like all human devices, however, the guide rope, along with its advantages, has its inconveniences. Its rubbing along the uneven

surfaces of the ground — over fields and meadows, hills and val-
leys, roads and houses, hedges and telegraph wires — gives violent
shocks to the balloon. Or it may happen that the guide rope, rapidly unraveling the snarl in which it has twisted itself, catches hold of
some asperity of the surface, or winds itself around the trunk or
branches of a tree. Such an incident was alone lacking to complete
my instruction.

As we passed a little group of trees, a shock stronger than any
hitherto felt threw us backward in the basket. The balloon had
stopped short and was swaying in the wind gusts at the end of its
guide rope, which had coiled itself around the head of an oak. For a
quarter of an hour it kept us shaking like a salad basket; and it was
only by throwing out a quantity of ballast that we finally got ourselves
loose. The lightened balloon made a tremendous leap upward and
pierced the clouds like a cannon ball. Indeed, it threatened to reach
dangerous heights, considering the little ballast we had remaining
in store for use in descending. It was time to have recourse to ef-
fective means — to open the maneuver valve and let out a portion
of our gas.

It was the work of a moment. The balloon began descending to
earth again, and soon the guide rope again rested on the ground.
There was nothing to do but to bring the trip to an end, because
only a few handfuls of sand remained to us.

He who wishes to navigate an airship should first practise a good
many landings in a spherical balloon — that is, if he wishes to land
without breaking balloon, keel, motor, rudder, propeller, water-
ballast cylinders, and fuel holders.

The wind being rather strong, it was necessary to seek shelter
for this last maneuver. At the end of the plain, a corner of the Forest of Fontainebleau was hurrying toward us. In a few moments
we had turned the extremity of the wood, sacrificing our last handful of ballast. The trees now protected us from the violence of the
wind; and we cast anchor, at the same time opening wide the emergency valve for the wholesale escape of the gas.

The twofold maneuver landed us without the least dragging. We
set foot on solid ground, and stood there, watching the balloon die.
Stretched out in the field, it was losing the remains of its gas in con-
vulsive agitations, like a great bird that dies beating its wings.

After taking a dozen instantaneous photographs of the dying
balloon, we folded it and packed it in the basket, with its netting

folded alongside. The little chosen corner in which we had landed formed part of the grounds of the Château de La Ferrière, belonging to M. Alphonse de Rothschild. Laborers from a neighboring field were sent for a conveyance to the village of La Ferrière itself, and half an hour later a break came. Putting everything into it, we set off to the railway station, which was some 2½ miles distant. There we had some work to lift the basket with its contents to the ground, as it weighed 440 pounds. At 6:30 we were back in Paris, after a journey of more than 60 miles and nearly two hours passed in the air.

CHAPTER IV

MY "BRAZIL," SMALLEST OF SPHERICAL BALLOONS

I liked ballooning so much that, coming back from my first trip with M. Machuron, I told him that I wanted a balloon built for myself. He liked the idea, but thought that I wanted an ordinary-sized spherical balloon, between 500 and 2000 cubic meters in volume. No one would think of making one smaller.

It is only a short time ago, but it is curious how constructors still clung to heavy materials. The smallest balloon-basket had to weigh 30 kilograms (66 pounds). Nothing was light — neither envelop, rigging, nor accessories.

I gave M. Machuron my ideas. He cried out against it when I told him I wanted a balloon of the lightest and toughest Japanese silk, 100 cubic meters (about 3500 cubic feet) in volume. At the works, both he and M. Lachambre tried to prove to me that the thing was impossible.

How often have things been proved to me impossible! Now I am used to it, I expect it. But in those days it troubled me. Still I persevered.

They showed me that for a balloon to have "stability," it must have a certain weight. Again, a balloon of 100 cubic meters, they said, would be affected by the movements of the aeronaut in his basket much more than a large balloon of regulation size.

With a large balloon the center of gravity in the weight of the aeronaut is as in Figure I, *a*. When the aeronaut moves, say, to the right in his basket, Figure I, *b*, the center of gravity of the whole system is not shifted appreciably.

In a very small balloon, the center of gravity, Figure 2, *a*, is undisturbed only so long as the aeronaut sits straight in the center of his basket. When he moves to the right the center of gravity, Figure 2, *b,* is shifted beyond the vertical line of the balloon's circumference, causing the balloon to swing in the same direction.

Therefore, they said, your necessary movements in the basket will cause your little balloon to roll and swing continually.

"We shall make the suspension tackle longer in proportion," I replied. It was done, and the "Brazil" proved remarkably stable.

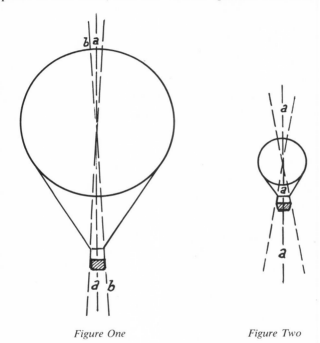

Figure One   *Figure Two*

When I brought my light Japanese silk to M. Lachambre, he looked at it and said: "It will be too weak." But when we came to try it with the dynamometer it surprised us. Tested thus, Chinese silk stands over 1000 kilograms (or 2200 pounds) strain to the linear meter (3.3 yards). The thin Japanese silk stood a strain of 700 kilograms (1540 pounds); that is, it proved to be thirty times stronger than necessary according to the theory of strains. This is astonishing when you consider that it weighs only 30 grams (a little more than one ounce) per square meter. To show how experts may be mistaken in their merely offhand judgments, I have been building my airship balloons of this same material; yet the inside pressure they have to stand is enormous, while all spherical balloons have a great hole in the bottom to relieve it.

As the proportions finally adopted for the "Brazil" were 113 cubic meters (4104 cubic feet), corresponding to about 113 square meters (135 square yards) of silk surface, the whole envelop weighed scarcely 3½ kilograms (less than 8 pounds). But the weight of the varnish — three coats — brought it up to 14 kilograms (about 31 pounds). The net, which often weighs into the hundreds of pounds, weighed 1800 grams, or nearly 4 pounds. The basket which usually weighs 30 kilograms (66 pounds) at a minimum, weighed 6 kilograms (13 pounds); the basket which I now have with my little "No. 9" weighs less than 5 kilograms (11 pounds). My guide rope, small, but very long — 100 yards — weighed at most 8 kilograms (17½ pounds); its length gave the "Brazil" a good spring. Instead of an anchor, I put in a little grappling iron of 3 kilograms (6½ pounds).

Making everything light in this way, I found that in spite of the smallness of the balloon, it would have ascensional force to take up my own weight of 50 kilograms (110 pounds) and 30 kilograms (66 pounds) of ballast. As a matter of fact, I took up that amount on my first trip. On another occasion, when a French cabinet minister was present, anxious to see the smallest spherical balloon ever made, I had practically no ballast at all — only 4 or 5 kilograms (10 or 11 pounds). Nevertheless, causing the balloon to be weighed, I went up and made a good ascent.

The "Brazil" was very handy in the air, easy to control. It was easy to pack also, on descending; and the story that I carried it in a valise is true.

Before starting out in my little "Brazil," I made from twenty-five to thirty ascents in ordinary spherical balloons, quite alone, as my own captain and sole passenger. M. Lachambre had many public ascents, and allowed me to do some of them for him. Thus I made ascents in many parts of France and Belgium. As I got the pleasure and the experience, and paid all my expenses and damages, it was a mutually advantageous arrangement.

I do not believe that, without such previous study and experience with a spherical balloon, a man can be capable of succeeding with an elongated dirigible balloon, whose handling is so much more delicate. Before attempting to direct an airship, it is necessary to

5. My "Brazil," smallest of the spherical balloons

6. The rooftops of Paris

have learned in an ordinary balloon the conditions of the atmospheric medium, to have become acquainted with the caprices of the wind, and to have gone thoroughly into the difficulties of the ballast problem from the triple point of view of starting, of equilibrium in the air, and of landing at the end of the trip.

To have been one's self the captain of an ordinary balloon at the very least a dozen times seems to me an indispensable preliminary to acquiring an exact notion of the requisites for constructing and handling an elongated balloon furnished with its motor and propeller.

Naturally I am filled with amazement when I see inventors who have never set foot in the basket drawing up on paper — and even executing in whole or in part — fantastic airships whose balloons are to have a capacity of thousands of cubic meters, loaded down with enormous motors which they do not succeed in raising from the ground, and furnished with machinery so complicated that nothing works! Such inventors are afraid of nothing, because they have no idea of the difficulties of the problem. Had they previously journeyed through the air at the wind's will and amid all the disturbing influence of atmospheric phenomena, they would understand that a dirigible balloon, to be practical, requires first of all to have the utmost extreme of simplicity in all its mechanism.

Some of the unhappy constructors who have paid with their lives the forfeit of their rashness had never made a single responsible ascent as captain of a spherical balloon. And the majority of their emulators, now so devotedly laboring, are in the same inexperienced condition. This is my explanation of their lack of success. They are in the condition in which the first-comer would find himself were he to agree to build and steer a transatlantic liner without having ever quitted land or set foot in a boat!

CHAPTER V

THE REAL AND THE IMAGINARY
DANGERS OF BALLOONING

One of the most astonishing adventures I had during this period of spherical ballooning took place directly over Paris.

I had started from Vaugirard, with four invited guests, in a large balloon constructed for me after I had tired of making solitary trips in the little "Brazil."

From the start there seemed to be very little wind. I rose slowly, seeking an air current. At 1000 meters (3/5 of a mile) high I found nothing. At 1500 meters (about one mile) we still remained almost stationary. Throwing out more ballast, we rose to 2000 meters (1¼ miles), when a vagrant breeze started to take us over the center of Paris.

When we had arrived at a point over the Louvre — it left us! We descended — and found nothing!

Then happened the ludicrous thing. In a blue sky without a cloud, bathed in sunlight, and with the faint yelps of all the dogs of Paris mounting to our ears, we lay becalmed! Up we went again, hunting an air current. Down we went again, hunting an air current. Up and down, up and down! Hour after hour passed; and we remained hanging always over Paris!

At first we laughed. Then we grew tired. Then almost alarmed. At one time I had even the idea of landing in Paris itself, near the Gare de Lyon, where I perceived an open space. Yet the attempt would have been dangerous, because my four companions could not be depended on for coolness in an emergency. They had not the ballooning habit.

Worst of all, we were now losing gas. Drifting slowly eastward hour after hour, one by one the sacks of ballast had been emptied.

By the time that we had reached the Vincennes wood we had begun to throw out miscellaneous objects — ballast sacks, the luncheon baskets, two light camp stools, two kodaks, and a case of photographic plates!

All during this latter period we were quite low — not over 300 yards above the tree tops. Now, as we sank lower, we had a real fright. Would not the guide rope at last curl itself around some tree and hold us there for hours? So we struggled to maintain our altitude above the tree tops, until all at once a queer little wind gust took us over the Vincennes racecourse.

"Now is our time!" I exclaimed to my companions. "Hold fast!"

With this I pulled on the valve rope, and we came down with celerity but scarcely any shock.

Personally, I have felt not only fear but also pain and real despair in a spherical balloon. It has not been often, because no sport is more regularly safe and mild and pleasurable. Such real dangers as it has are confined usually to the landing, and the balloonist of experience knows how to meet them; while from its imaginary dangers in the air one is regularly very safe. Therefore the particular adventure full of pain and fear that I recall to mind was all the more remarkable in that it occurred in high altitude.

It happened at Nice in 1900, when I went up from the Place Masséna in a good-sized spherical balloon, alone, and intending to drift a few hours only amid the enchanting scenery of the mountains and the sea.

The weather was fine, but the barometer soon fell, indicating storm. For a time the wind took me in the direction of Cimiez, but as I rose it threatened to carry me out to sea. I threw out ballast, abandoned the current, and mounted to the height of about a mile.

Shortly after this I let the balloon go down again, hoping to find a safe air current, but when within 300 yards of the ground, near the Var, I noticed that I had ceased descending. As I had determined to land soon in any case, I pulled on the valve rope and let out more gas. And here the terrible experience began!

I could not go down! I glanced at the barometer and found, indeed, that I was going up! Yet I ought to be descending, and I felt — by the wind and everything — that I must be descending! Had I not let out gas?

To my great uneasiness I discovered only too soon what was wrong. In spite of my continuous apparent descent, I was, nevertheless, being lifted by an enormous column of air rushing upward! While I fell in it I rose rapidly higher with it!

I opened the valve again. It was useless. The barometer showed that I had reached a still greater altitude, and I could now take account of the fact by the way in which the land was disappearing under me. I now closed the valve to save my gas. There was nothing but to wait and see what would happen.

The upward-rushing column of air continued to take me to a height of 3000 meters (almost two miles). I could do nothing but watch the barometer. Then, after what seemed a long time, it showed that I had begun descending.

When I began to see land, I threw out ballast, not to strike the earth too quickly. Now I could perceive the storm beating the trees and shrubbery. Up in the storm itself I had felt nothing.

Now, too, as I continued falling lower, I could see how swiftly I was being carried laterally. By the time I perceived the coming danger I was in it. Carried along at a terrific rate, knocking against the tops of trees and continually threatened with a painful death, I threw out my anchor. It caught in trees and shrubs and broke away. Had it been heavy timber, all would have been over with me. As it chanced, I was dragged through the small trees and yielding shrubbery, my face a mass of cuts and bruises, my clothes torn from my back, in pain and strain, fearing the worst and able to do nothing to save myself! Just as I had given myself up for lost, the guide rope wound itself around a tree and held. I was precipitated from the basket and fell unconscious. When I came to, I had to walk several miles until I found some peasants. They helped me back to Nice, where I went to bed and had the doctors sew me up.

During the early period when I was glad to make public ascents for my balloon constructor, I had undergone a somewhat similar experience, and that by night. The ascent took place at Péronne, in the north of France, one stormy afternoon, quite late. Indeed, I started in spite of thunder threatening in the distance, a gloomy, semi-twilight all around me, and the remonstrances of the public, among whom it was known that I was not an aeronaut by trade. They feared my inexperience, and wished me either to renounce the ascent or else to oblige me to take up the balloon constructor with me, he being the responsible organizer of the *fête*.

I would listen to nothing, and started off as I had planned. Soon I had cause to regret my rashness. I was alone, lost in the clouds, amid flashes of lightning and claps of thunder, in the rapidly approaching darkness of the night!

On, on I went tearing in the blackness. I knew that I must be going with great speed, yet felt no motion. I heard and felt the storm. I formed a part of the storm! I felt myself in great danger, yet the danger was not tangible. With it there was a fierce kind of joy. What shall I say? How shall I describe it? Up there in the black solitude, amid the lightning flashes and the thunderclaps, I was a part of the storm!

When I landed the next morning — long after I had sought a higher altitude and let the storm pass on beneath me — I found that I was well into Belgium. The dawn was peaceful, so that my landing took place without difficulty. I mention this adventure because it was made account of in the papers of the time, and to show that night ballooning, even in a storm, may be more dangerous in appearance than in reality. Indeed, night ballooning has a charm that is all its own.

One is alone in the black void, true, in a murky limbo where one seems to float without weight, without a surrounding world, a soul freed from the weight of matter! Yet, now and again there are the lights of earth to cheer one. We see a point of light far on ahead. Slowly it expands. Then where there was one blaze, there are countless bright spots. They run in lines, with here and there a brighter cluster. We know that it is a city.

Then, again, it is out into the lone land, with only a faint glow here and there. When the moon rises we see, perhaps, a faint curling line of gray. It is a river, with the moonlight falling on its waters.

There is a flash upward and a faint roar. It is a railway train, the locomotive's fires, maybe, illuminating for a moment its smoke as it rises.

Then, for safety, we throw out more ballast and rise through the black solitudes of the clouds into a soul-lifting burst of splendid starlight. There, alone with the constellations, we await the dawn!

And when the dawn comes, red and gold and purple in its glory, one is almost loath to seek the earth again, although the novelty of landing in who knows what part of Europe affords still another unique pleasure.

For many the great charm of all ballooning lies here. The balloonist becomes an explorer. Say that you are a young man who would roam, who would enjoy adventures, who would penetrate the unknown and deal with the unexpected; but say that you are tied down at home by family and business. I advise you to take to spherical ballooning. At noon you lunch peaceably amid your family. At 2 P.M. you mount. Ten minutes later you are no longer a commonplace citizen — you are an explorer, an adventurer of the unknown as truly as they who freeze on Greenland's icy mountains or melt on India's coral strands.

You know but vaguely where you are, and cannot know where you are going. Yet much may depend upon your choice as well as your skill and experience. The choice of altitude is yours, whether to accept this current or mount higher and go with another. You may mount above the clouds, where one breathes oxygen from tubes, while the earth, in the last glimpse you had of it, seems to spin beneath you and you lose all bearings; or you may descend and scud along the surface, aided by your guide rope and a dipperful of ballast to leap over trees and houses — giant leaps made without effort!

Then, when the time comes to land, there is the true explorer's zest of coming on unknown peoples like a god from a machine. "What country is this?" Will the answer come in German, Russian, or Norwegian? Paris Aéro Club members have been shot at when crossing European frontiers! Others, landing, have been taken prisoners to the burgomaster or the military governor, to languish as spies while the telegraph clicked to the far-off capital, and then to end the evening over champagne at an officers' enthusiastic mess! Still others have had to strive with the dangerous ignorance, and superstition even, of some remote little peasant population! These are the chances of the winds!

CHAPTER VI

I YIELD TO THE STEERABLE BALLOON IDEA

During my ascent with M. Machuron, while our guide rope was wrapped around the tree and the wind was shaking us so outrageously, he improved the occasion to discourage me against all steerable ballooning.

"Observe the treachery and vindictiveness of the wind!" he cried between shocks. "We are tied to the tree, yet see with what force it tries to jerk us loose!" [Here I was thrown again into the bottom of the basket.] "What screw propeller could hold a course against it? What elongated balloon would not double up and take you flying to destruction?"

It was discouraging. Returning to Paris by rail, I gave up the ambition to continue Giffard's trials, and this state of mind lasted with me for weeks. I would have argued fluently against the dirigibility of balloons! Then came a new period of temptation, for a long-cherished idea dies hard. When I took account of its practical difficulties, I found my mind working automatically to convince itself that they were not. I caught myself saying: "If I make a cylindrical balloon long enough and thin enough, it will cut the air . . . " and, with respect to the wind: "Shall I not be as a sailing yachtsman who is not criticized for refusing to go out in a squall?"

At last an accident decided me. I have always been charmed by simplicity, while complications, be they never so ingenious, repel me. Automobile tricycle motors happened to be very much perfected at the moment. I delighted in their simplicity, and, illogically enough, their merits had the effect of deciding my mind against all other objections to steerable ballooning.

"I will use this light and powerful motor," I said. "Giffard had no such opportunity!"

Giffard's primitive steam engine, weak in proportion to its weight, spitting red-hot sparks from its coal fuel, had afforded that courageous innovator no fair chance, I argued. I did not dally a single moment with the idea of an electric motor, which promises little danger, it is true, but which has the capital ballooning defect of being the heaviest known engine, counting the weight of its battery. Indeed, that I shall say no more about it except to repeat what Mr. Edison said to me on this head in April, 1902. "You have done well," he said, "to choose the petroleum motor. It is the only one of which an aeronaut can dream in the present state of the industry; and steerable balloons with electric motors, especially as they were fifteen or twenty years ago, could have led to no result. That is why the Tissandier brothers gave them up."

In spite of the recent immense improvements made in the steam engine, it would not have been able to decide me in favor of steerable ballooning. Motor for motor it is, perhaps, better than the petroleum motor, but when you compare the boiler with the carburetor, the latter weighs grams per horsepower while the boiler weighs kilograms. In certain light steam motors that are lighter, even, than petroleum motors, the boiler always ruins the proportion. With one pound of petroleum you can exert one horsepower during one hour. To get this same energy from the most improved steam engine you will want many kilograms of water and of fuel, be it petroleum or other. Even condensing the water, you cannot have less than several kilograms per horsepower.

Then, if you use coal fuel with the steam motor, there are the burning sparks; while if you use petroleum with burners, you have a great amount of fire. We must do the petroleum motor the justice to admit that it makes neither flame nor burning sparks!

At the present moment I have a Clément petroleum motor that weighs but 2 kilograms (4½ pounds) per horsepower. This is my 60 horsepower "No. 7," whose total weight is but 120 kilograms (264 pounds). Compare this with the new steel-and-nickel battery of Mr. Edison, which promises to weigh 18 kilograms (40 pounds) per horsepower!

The light weight and the simplicity of the little tricycle motor of 1897 are, therefore, responsible for all my trials! I started from this principle: to make any kind of success, it would be necessary to economize weight and so comply with the pecuniary as well as the mechanical conditions of the problem.

Nowadays I build airships in a large way. I am in it as a kind of lifework. Then I was but a half-decided beginner, unwilling to spend large sums of money in a doubtful project.

Therefore I resolved to build an elongated balloon, just large enough to raise, along with my own one hundred and ten pounds of weight, as much more as might be necessary for the basket and rigging, motor, fuel, and absolutely indispensable ballast. In reality I was building an airship to fit my little tricycle motor!

I looked for the workshop of some small mechanic near my residence in the center of residential Paris, where I could have my plans executed under my own eyes and could apply my own hands to the task. I found such a one in the Rue du Colisée. There I first worked out a tandem of two cylinders of a tricycle motor — that is, their prolongation one after the other to work the same connecting rod while fed by a single carburetor.

To bring everything down to a minimum weight, I cut out from every part of the motor whatever was not strictly necessary to solidity. In this way I realized something that was interesting in those days — a 3½ horsepower motor that weighed 30 kilograms (66 pounds).

I soon had an opportunity to test my tandem motor. The great series of automobile road races, which seems to have had its climax in Paris – Madrid in 1903, was raising the power of these wonderful engines by leaps and bounds year after year. Paris-Bordeaux in 1895 was won with a 4 horsepower machine at an average speed of 25 kilometers (15½ miles) per hour. In 1896 Paris-Marseilles-and-return was accomplished at the rate of 30 kilometers (18½ miles) per hour. Now in 1897 it was Paris-Amsterdam. Although not entered for the race, it occurred to me to try my tandem motor attached to its original tricycle. I started, and, to my contentment, found that I could keep well up with the pace. Indeed, I might have won a good place in the finish — my vehicle was the most powerful of the lot in proportion to its weight, and the average speed of the winner was only 40 kilometers (25 miles) per hour — had I not begun to fear that the jarring of my motor in so strenuous an effort might in the long run derange it, and I imagined I had more important work for it to do.

For that matter, my automobiling experience has stood me in good stead with my airships. The petroleum motor is still a delicate and capricious thing, and there are sounds in its spitting rumble

that are intelligible only to the long-experienced ear. Should the
time come in some future flight of mine when the motor of my airship threatens danger, I am convinced that my ear will hear, and
I shall heed the warning. This almost instinctive faculty I owe only
to experience. Having broken up the tricycle for the sake of its motor, I purchased at about this time an up-to-date 6 horsepower
Panhard, with which I went from Paris to Nice in 54 hours, night
and day, without stop; and had I not taken up dirigible ballooning,
I must have become a road-racing automobile enthusiast, continually exchanging one type for another, continually in search of
greater speed, keeping pace with the progress of the industry, as
so many others do, to the glory of French mechanics and the new
Parisian sporting spirit.

But my airships stopped me. While experimenting I was tied
down to Paris. I could take no long trips, and the petroleum automobile, with its wonderful facility for finding fuel in every hamlet,
lost its greatest use in my eyes. In 1898 I happened to see what
was to me an unknown make of light American electric buggy. It
appealed alike to my eye, my needs, and my reason, and I bought
it. I have never had cause to regret the purchase. It serves me for
running about Paris, and it goes lightly, noiselessly, and without
odor.

I had already handed the plan of my balloon envelop to the constructors. It was that of a cylindrical balloon terminating fore and
aft in cones 25 meters (82½ feet) long, with a diameter of 3.5 meters
(11½ feet) and a gas capacity of 180 cubic meters (6354 cubic feet).
My calculations had left me only 30 kilograms (66 pounds) for
both the balloon material and its varnish. Therefore I gave up the
usual network and *chemise,* or outer cover; indeed, I considered
this second envelop, holding the balloon proper within it, to be not
only superfluous but harmful, if not dangerous. Instead, I attached
the suspension cords of my basket directly to the balloon envelop
by means of small wooden rods introduced into long horizontal
hems sewed on both sides to its stuff for a great part of the balloon's length. Again, in order not to pass my 66 pounds including
varnish, I was obliged to have recourse to my Japanese silk, which
had proved so staunch in the "Brazil."

After glancing at this order for the balloon envelop, M. Lachambre at first refused it plumply. He would not make himself a
party to such rashness. But when I recalled to his memory how he

had said the same thing with respect to the "Brazil," and went on to assure him that, if necessary, I would cut and sew the balloon with my own hands, he gave way to me and undertook the job. He would cut and sew and varnish the balloon according to my plans.

The balloon envelop being thus put under way, I prepared my basket, motor, propeller, rudder, and machinery. When they were completed I made many trials with them, suspending the whole system by a cord from the rafters of the workshop, starting the motor, and measuring the force of the forward swing caused by the propeller working on the atmosphere behind it. Holding back this forward movement by means of a horizontal rope attached to a dy-

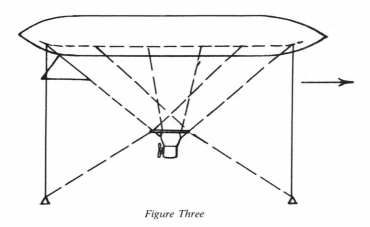

Figure Three

namometer, I found that the traction power developed by the motor in my propeller, with two arms each measuring one meter across, to be as high as 11.4 kilograms (25 pounds). This was a figure that promised good speed to a cylindrical balloon of my dimensions, whose length was equal to nearly seven times its diameter. With 1200 turns to the minute, the propeller — which was attached directly to the motor shaft — might easily, if all went well, give the airship a speed of not less than 26½ feet per second.

The rudder I made of silk stretched over a triangular steel frame. There now remained nothing to devise but a system of shifting weights, which, from the very first, I saw would be indispensable. For this purpose I placed two bags of ballast, one fore and one aft, suspended from the balloon envelop by cords. By means of lighter cords each of these two weights could be drawn into the basket (see Figure 3), thus shifting the center of gravity of the whole system. Pulling in the fore weight would cause the stem of the balloon to point diagonally upward; pulling in the aft weight would have just the opposite effect. Besides these, I had a guide rope some 60 meters (200 feet) long, which could also be used, at need, as shifting ballast.

All this occupied several months, and the work was all carried on in the little machine shop of the Rue du Colisée, only a few steps from the place where, later, the Paris Aéro Club was to have its first offices.

CHAPTER VII

MY FIRST AIRSHIP CRUISES (1898)

In the middle of September, 1898, I was ready to begin in the open air. The rumor had spread among the aeronauts of Paris, who formed the nucleus of the Aéro Club, that I was going to carry up a petroleum motor in my basket. They were sincerely disquieted by what they called my temerity, and some of them made friendly efforts to show me the permanent danger of such a motor under a balloon filled with a highly inflammable gas. They begged me, instead, to use the electric motor — "which is infinitely less dangerous."

I had arranged to inflate the balloon at the Jardin d'Acclimatation, where a captive balloon was already installed and furnished with everything needful daily. This gave me facilities for obtaining, at one franc per cubic meter, the 180 cubic meters (6354 cubic feet) of hydrogen which I needed.

On September 18 my first airship — the "Santos-Dumont No. 1," as it has since been called to distinguish it from those which followed — lay stretched out on the turf amid the trees of the beautiful Jardin d'Acclimatation, the new Zoological Garden of the west of Paris. To understand what happened, I must explain the starting of spherical balloons from such places, where groups of trees and other obstructions surround the open space.

When the weighing and balancing of the balloon are finished, and the aeronauts have taken their place in the basket, the balloon is ready to quit the ground with a certain ascensional force. Thereupon aids carry it toward an extremity of the open space in the direction from which the wind happens to be blowing, and it is there that the order, "Let go, all!" is given. In this way the balloon has the entire open space to cross before reaching the trees or other ob-structions which may be opposite and toward which the wind would naturally carry it. So it has space and time to rise high enough to pass over them. Moreover, the ascensional force of the balloon is regulated accordingly: it is very little if the wind be light; it is more if the wind be stronger.

I had thought that my airship would be able to go against the wind that was then blowing; therefore, I had intended to place it for the start at precisely the other end of the open space from that which I have described: that is, downstream, and not upstream in the air current, with relation to the open space surrounded by trees. I would thus move out of the open space without difficulty, having the wind against me — for, under such conditions, the relative speed of the airship ought to be the difference between its absolute speed and the velocity of the wind — and so by going against the air current I should have plenty of time to rise and pass over the trees. Evidently it would be a mistake to place the airship at a point suitable for an ordinary balloon without motor and propeller.

And yet it was there that I did place it — not by my own will, but by the will of the professional aeronauts who came in the crowd to be present at my experiment. In vain I explained that, by placing myself "upstream" in the wind with relation to the center of the open space, I should inevitably risk precipitating the airship against the trees before I should have time to rise above them, the speed of my propeller being superior to that of the wind then blowing.

All was useless. The aeronauts had never seen a dirigible balloon start off. They could not admit of its starting under other conditions than those of a spherical balloon, in spite of the essential difference between the two. As I was alone against them all, I had the weakness to yield.

I started off from the very spot they indicated, and within a second's time I tore my airship against the trees, as I had feared I should do. After this, deny, if you can, the existence of a fulcrum in the air!

This accident at least served to show the effectiveness of my motor and propeller in the air to those who doubted it before.

I did not waste time in regrets. Two days later, on September 20, I actually started from the same open space — this time choosing my own starting point.

I passed over the tops of the trees without mishap, and at once

7. The "Santos-Dumont No. 1"

8. Motor of the "Santos-Dumont No. 1"

began sailing around them, to give on the spot a first demonstration of the airship to the great crowd of Parisians that had assembled. I had their sympathy and applause then, as I have had them ever since; the Parisian public has always been a kind and enthusiastic witness of my efforts.

Under the combined action of the propeller impulse, of the steering rudder, of the displacement of the guide rope, and of the two sacks of ballast sliding backward and forward as I willed, I had the satisfaction of making my evolutions in every direction — to right and left, and up and down.

Such a result encouraged me, and, being inexperienced, I made the great mistake of mounting high in the air — to 400 meters (1300 feet) — an altitude that is considered nothing for a spherical balloon, but which is absurd and uselessly dangerous for an airship under trial.

At this height I commanded a view of all the monuments of Paris. I continued my evolutions in the direction of the Longchamps racecourse, which from that day I chose for the scene of my aerial experiments.

So long as I continued to ascend, the hydrogen increased in volume as a consequence of the atmospheric depression. So by its tension the balloon was kept taut, and everything went well. It was not the same when I began descending. The air pump, which was intended to compensate the contraction of the hydrogen, was of insufficient capacity. The balloon, a long cylinder, all at once began to fold in the middle like a pocket knife, the tension of the cords became unequal, and the balloon envelop was on the point of being torn by them. At that moment I thought that all was over; the more so as the descent which had begun could no longer be checked by any of the usual means on board, where nothing worked.

The descent became a fall. Luckily, I was falling in the neighborhood of the grassy turf of Bagatelle, where some big boys were flying kites. A sudden idea struck me. I cried to them to grasp the end of my guide rope, which had already touched the ground, and to run as fast as they could with it *against the wind!*

They were bright young fellows, and they grasped the idea and the rope at the same lucky instant. The effect of this help *in extremis* was immediate and such as I had hoped. By the maneuver we lessened the velocity of the fall, and so avoided what would otherwise have been a bad shaking up, to say the least.

I was saved for the first time! Thanking the brave boys, who continued aiding me to pack everything into the airship's basket, I finally secured a cab and took the relics back to Paris.

.

CHAPTER VIII

HOW IT FEELS TO NAVIGATE
THE AIR

Notwithstanding the breakdown, I felt nothing but elation that night. The sentiment of success filled me. I had navigated the air.

I had performed every evolution prescribed by the problem. *The breakdown itself had not been due to any cause foreseen by the professional aeronauts.*

I had mounted without sacrificing ballast. I had descended without sacrificing gas. My shifting weights had proved successful, and it would have been impossible not to recognize the capital triumph of these oblique flights through the air. No one had ever made them before.

Of course, when starting, or shortly after leaving the ground, one has sometimes to throw out ballast to balance the machine, as one may have made a mistake and started with the airship far too heavy. What I have referred to is maneuvers in the air.

My first impression of aerial navigation was, I confess, surprise to feel the airship going straight ahead. It was astonishing to feel the wind in my face. In spherical ballooning we go with the wind and do not feel it. True, in rising and descending the spherical balloonist feels the friction of the atmosphere, and the vertical oscillation makes the flag flutter, but in the horizontal movement the ordinary balloon seems to stand still while the earth flies past under it.

As my airship plowed ahead, the wind struck my face and fluttered my coat as on the deck of a transatlantic liner, though in other respects it will be more accurate to liken aerial to river navigation with a steamboat. It is not like sail navigation, and all talk about "tacking" is meaningless. If there is any wind at all, it is in a given direction, so that the analogy with a river current is complete. When there is no wind at all, we may liken it to the navigation of a smooth lake or pond. It will be well to understand this matter.

Suppose that my motor and propeller push me through the air at the rate of 20 miles an hour. I am in the position of a steamboat captain whose propeller is driving him up or down the river at the rate of 20 miles an hour. Imagine the current to be 10 miles per hour. If he navigates against the current, he accomplishes 10 miles an hour with respect to the shore, though he has been traveling at the rate of 20 miles an hour through the water. If he goes with the current, he accomplishes 30 miles an hour with respect to the shore, though he has not been going any faster through the water. This is one of the reasons why it is so difficult to estimate the speed of an airship.

It is also the reason why airship captains will always prefer to navigate for their own pleasure in calm weather, and, when they find an air current against them, will steer obliquely upward or downward to get out of it. Birds do the same thing. The sailing yachtsman whistles for a fair breeze, without which he can do nothing; but the river steamboat captain will always hug the shore to avoid the freshet, and will time his descent of the river by the outgoing rather than the incoming tide. We airshipmen are steamboat captains and not sailing yachtsmen.

The navigator of the air, however, has one great advantage — he can leave one current for another. The air is full of varying currents. Mounting, he will find an advantageous breeze or else a calm. These are strictly practical considerations, having nothing to do with the airship's ability to battle with the breeze when obliged to do it.

Before going on my first trip, I had wondered if I should be seasick. I foresaw that the sensation of mounting and descending obliquely with my shifting weights might be unpleasant. And I looked forward to a good deal of pitching *(tangage)*, as they say on board ship. Of rolling there would not be so much. But both sensations would be novel in ballooning, for the spherical balloon gives no sensation of movement at all.

In my first airship, however, the suspension was very long, approximating that of a spherical balloon. For this reason there was very little pitching. And, speaking generally, since that time, though

I have been told that on this or that trip my airship pitched considerably, I have never been seasick. It may be due in part to the fact that I am rarely subject to this ill upon the water. Back and forth between Brazil and France, and between France and the United States, I have had experience of all kinds of weather. Once, on the way to Brazil, the storm was so violent that the grand piano went loose and broke a lady's leg; yet I was not seasick.

I know that what one feels most distressingly at sea is not so much the movement as that momentary hesitation just before the boat pitches, followed by the malicious dipping or mounting, which never comes quite the same, and the shock at top and bottom. All this is powerfully aided by the smells of the paint, varnish, and tar, mingled with the odors of the kitchen, the heat of the boilers, and the stench of the smoke and the hold.

In the airship there is no smell. All is pure and clean. And the pitching itself has none of the shocks and hesitations of the boat at sea. The movement is suave and flowing, which is doubtless owing to the lesser resistance of the airwaves. The pitches are less frequent and rapid than those at sea; the dip is not brusquely arrested, so that the mind can anticipate the curve to its end; and there is no shock to give that queer "empty" sensation to the solar plexus.

Furthermore, the shocks of a transatlantic liner are due first to the fore and then to the after part of the giant construction rising out of the water to plunge into it again. The airship never leaves its medium — the air — in which it only swings.

This consideration brings me to the most remarkable of all the sensations of aerial navigation. This is the utterly new sensation of movement in an extra dimension. On my first trip it actually shocked me!

Man has never known anything like free vertical existence. Held to the plane of the earth, his movement "down" has scarcely been more than to return to it after a short excursion "up," our minds remaining always on the plane surface even while our bodies may be mounting; and this is so much the case that the spherical balloonist, as he rises, has no sense of movement, but gains the impression that the earth is descending below him.

With respect of combinations of vertical and horizontal movements, man is absolutely without experience. Therefore, as all our sensations of movement are practically in two dimensions, it is the extraordinary novelty of aerial navigation that it affords us experiences — not in the fourth dimension, it is true — but in what is practically an extra dimension, the third, so that the miracle is similar. Indeed, I cannot describe the delight, the wonder, and intoxication of this free diagonal movement onward and upward, or onward and downward, combined at will with brusque changes of direction horizontally when the airship answers to a touch of the rudder! The birds have this sensation when they spread their wings and go tobogganing in curves and spirals through the sky.

"Por mares nunca d'antes navegados!"
(O'er seas heretofore unsailed!)

The line of our great poet echoed in my memory from childhood. After this first of all my cruises, I had it put on my flag.

It is true that spherical ballooning had prepared me for the mere sensation of height; but that is a very different matter. It is therefore curious that, prepared as I was on this score, the mere thought of height should have given me my only unpleasant experience. What I mean is this:

The wonderful new combinations of vertical and horizontal movements, utterly out of previous human experience, caused me neither surprise nor trouble. I would find myself plowing diagonally upward through the air with a kind of instinctive liberty. And yet when moving horizontally — as you would say, in the natural position — a glance downward at the housetops disquieted me.

"What if I should fall?" the thought came. The housetops looked so dangerous, with their chimney pots for spikes! One seldom has this thought in a spherical balloon, because we know that the danger in the air is nil: the great spherical balloon can neither suddenly lose its gas nor burst. My little airship balloon had to support not only exterior but interior pressure as well, which is not the case with a spherical balloon, as I shall explain in the next chapter; and any injury to the cylindrical form of any airship balloon by loss of gas might prove fatal.

While over the housetops I felt that it would be bad to fall; but as soon as I left Paris and was navigating over the forests of the Bois de Boulogne, the idea left me entirely. Below there seemed to be a great ocean of greenery, soft and safe.

It was while over the continuation of this greenery in the grassy *pelouse* of the Longchamps racecourse that my balloon, having lost a great deal of its gas, began to double on itself. Previously I had heard a noise. Looking up, I saw that the long cylinder of the balloon was beginning to break. Then I was astonished and troubled. I wondered what I could do.

I could not think of anything to do. I might throw out ballast. That would cause the airship to rise, and the decreased pressure of the atmosphere would doubtless permit the expanding gas to straighten out the balloon again, taut and strong. But I remembered that I must always come down again when all the danger would repeat itself, and worse even then before, from the more gas I would have lost. There was nothing to do but to go on down instantly.

I remember having the sure idea: "If that balloon cylinder doubles any more, the ropes by which I am suspended to it will work at different strengths and will begin to break, one by one as I go down."

For the moment I was sure that I was in the presence of death. Well, I will tell it frankly, my sentiment was almost entirely that of waiting and expectation.

"What is coming next?" I thought. "What am I going to see and know in a few minutes? Whom shall I see after I am dead?"

The thought that I would be meeting my father in a few minutes thrilled me. Indeed, I think that in such moments there is no room for either regret or terror. The mind is too full of looking forward. One is frightened only so long as one still has a chance.

CHAPTER IX

EXPLOSIVE ENGINES AND INFLAMMABLE GASES

I have been so often and so sincerely warned against what is taken for granted to be the patent danger of operating explosive engines under masses of inflammable gases, that I may be pardoned for stopping a moment to disclaim undue or thoughtless rashness.

Very naturally, from the first the question of physical danger to myself called for consideration. I was the interested party, and I tried to view the question from all points. Well, the outcome of these meditations was to make me fear fire very little, while doubting other possibilities against which no one ever dreamed of warning me.

I remember that while working on the first of all my airships in that little carpenter shop of the Rue du Colisée I used to wonder how the vibrations of the petroleum motor would affect the system when it got in the air.

In those days we did not have the noiseless automobiles, free from vibration, of the present. Nowadays even the colossal 80- and 90- horsepower motors of the latest racing types can be started and stopped as gently as those great steel hammers in iron foundries, whose engineers make a trick of cracking the top of an egg with them without breaking the rest of the shell.

My tandem motor of two cylinders, working the same connecting-rod and fed by a single carburetor, realized 3½ horsepower — at that time a considerable force for its weight — and I had no idea how it would act off *terra firma*. I had seen motors "jump" along the highway. What would mine do in its little basket that weighed almost nothing and suspended from a balloon that weighed less than nothing?

You know the principle of these motors. One may say that there is gasoline in a receptacle. Air, passing through it, comes out mixed with gasoline gas, ready to explode. You give a whirl to a crank, and the thing begins working automatically. The piston goes down, sucking combined gas and air into the cylinder. Then the piston comes back and compresses it. At that moment an electric spark is struck. An explosion follows instantly, and the piston goes down, producing work. Then it goes up, throwing out the product of combustion. Thus, with the two cylinders there was one explosion for every turn of the shaft.

Wishing to have my mind clear on the question, I took my tricycle, just as it was after I had left the Paris-Amsterdam race, and, accompanied by a capable companion, I steered it to a lonely part of the Bois de Boulogne. There in the forest I chose a great tree with low hanging limbs. From two of them we suspended the motor-tricycle by three ropes.

When we had well established the suspension, my companion aided me to climb up and seat myself on the tricycle saddle. I was as in a swing. In a moment I would start the motor and learn something of my future success or failure.

Would the vibration of the explosive engine shake me back and forth, strain at the ropes until it had unequalized their tension, and then break them one by one? Would it jar the interior air balloon's pump and derange the big balloon's valves? Would it continually jerk and pull at the silk hems and the thin rods which were to hold my basket to the balloon? Free from the steadying influence of the solid ground, would the jumping motor jar itself until it broke? And, breaking, might it not explode?

All this and more had been predicted by the professional aeronauts, and I had as yet no proof outside of reasoning that they might not be right on this or that topic.

I started the motor. I felt no particular vibration, and I was certainly not being shaken. I increased the speed — and felt *less* vibration! There could be no doubt about it: there was less vibration in this light weight tricycle hanging in the air than I had regularly felt while traveling on the ground. It was my first triumph in the air!

I will say frankly that as I rose in the air on my first trip I had no fear of fire. What I feared was that the balloon might burst by reason of its interior pressure. I still fear it.

Before going up I had minutely tried the valves. I still try them minutely before each of my trips. The danger, of course, was that the valves might not work adequately, in which case the expanding of the gas as the balloon rose would cause the dreaded explosion. Here is the great difference between spherical and dirigible balloons. The spherical balloon is always open. When it is taut with gas it is shaped like an apple; when it has lost part of its gas, it takes the shape of a pear; but in each case there is a great hole in the bottom of the spherical balloon — where the stem of the apple or the pear would be — and it is through this hole that the gas has opportunity to ease itself in the constant alternations of condensation and dilatation. Having such a free vent, the spherical balloon runs no risk of bursting in the air; but the price paid for this immunity is great loss of gas and, consequently, a fatal shortening of the spherical balloon's stay in the air. Someday a spherical balloonist will close up that hole. Indeed, they already talk of doing it.

I was obliged to do it in my airship balloon, whose cylindrical form must be preserved at all cost. For me there must be no transformations as from apple to pear. Interior pressure only could guarantee me this. The valves to which I refer have since my first experiments been of all kinds, some very ingeniously interacting, others of extreme simplicity. But their object in each case has been the same — to hold the gas tight in the balloon up to a certain pressure, and then to let out only enough to relieve dangerous interior pressure. It is easy to realize, therefore, that should these valves refuse to act adequately, the danger of bursting would be there.

This possible danger I acknowledged to myself, but it had nothing to do with fire from the explosive motor. Yet during all my preparations, and up to the moment of calling, "Let go, all!" the professional aeronauts, completely overlooking this weak point of the airship, continued to warn me against fire, of which I had no fear at all.

"Do we dare strike matches in the basket of a spherical balloon?" they asked.

"Do we even permit ourselves the solace of a cigarette on trips that last for many hours?"

To me the cases did not seem the same. In the first place, why should one not light a match in the basket of a spherical balloon? If it be only because the mind vaguely connects the ideas of gas and flame, the danger remains ideal. If it be because of a real possibility of igniting gas that has escaped from the free hole in the stem of the spherical balloon, it would not apply to me. My balloon, hermetically closed except when excessive pressure should let either air or a very little gas escape through one of the automatic valves, might for a moment leave a little trail of gas *behind* it as it moved on horizontally or diagonally, but there would be none in front where the motor was. (Figure 4.)

In this first airship I had placed the gas escape valves even farther from the motor than I place them today. The suspension cords being very long, I hung in my basket far below the balloon. Therefore I asked myself:

"How could this motor, so far below the balloon and so far in front of its escape valves, set fire to the gas inclosed in it when such gas is not inflammable until mixed with air?"

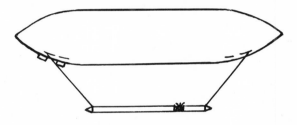

Figure Four

On this first trial, as in most since, I used hydrogen gas. Undoubtedly when mixed with air it is tremendously inflammable. But it must first mix with air. All my little balloon models are kept filled with hydrogen; and, so filled, I have more than once amused myself by burning *inside them,* not their hydrogen, but its mixture with the oxygen of the atmosphere. All one has to do is to insert in the balloon model a little tube to furnish a jet of the room's atmosphere from an air pump and light it with the electric spark. Similarly, should a pinprick have made ever so slight a vent in my airship balloon, the interior pressure would have sent out into the atmosphere a long, thin stream of hydrogen that *might* have ignited — had there been any flame near enough to do it. But there was none.

This was the problem. My motor did undoubtedly send out flames for, say, half a yard round about it. They were, however, mere flames, not still-burning products of incomplete combustion like the sparks of a steam engine. This admitted, how was the fact that I had a mass of hydrogen unmixed with air and well secured in a tight envelop so high above the motor to prove dangerous?

Turning the matter over and over in my mind, I could see but one dangerous possibility from fire. This was the possibility of the petroleum reservoir itself taking fire by a *retour de flamme* from the motor. During five years, I may here say in passing, I enjoyed complete immunity from the *retour de flamme* (sucking back of the flame). Then, in the same week in which Mr. Vanderbilt burned himself so severely, on July 6, 1903, the same accident overtook me in my little "No. 9" runabout airship just as I was crossing the Seine to land on the Île de Puteaux. I promptly extinguished the flame with my Panama hat, without other incident.

For reasons like these I went up on my first airship trip without fear of fire, but not without doubt of a possible explosion due to insufficient working of my balloon's escape valves. Should such a "cold" explosion occur, the flame-spitting motor would probably ignite the mass of mixed hydrogen and air that would surround me. But it would have no decisive influence on the result. The "cold" explosion itself would be sufficient.

Now, after five years of experience, and in spite of the *retour de flamme* above the Ile de Puteaux, I continue to regard the danger from fire as practically nil; but the possibility of a "cold" explosion remains always with me, and I must continue to purchase immunity from it at the cost of vigilant attention to my gas escape valves. Indeed, the possibility of the thing is greater, technically, now than in the early days which I describe. My first airship was not built for speed; consequently, it needed very little interior pressure to preserve the shape of its balloon. Now that I have great speed, as in my "No. 7," I must have enormous interior pressure to withstand the exterior pressure of the atmosphere in front of the balloon as I drive against it.

9.   *Retour de flamme* over the Ile de Puteaux

10. First start in the "Santos-Dumont No. 2"

CHAPTER X

I GO IN FOR AIRSHIP BUILDING

In the early spring of 1899 I built another airship, which the Paris public at once called the "Santos-Dumont No. 2." It had the same length and, at first sight, the same form as the "No. I", but its greater diameter brought its volume up to 200 cubic meters (over 7000 cubic feet) and gave me 20 kilograms (44 pounds) more ascensional force. I had taken account of the insufficiency of the air pump that had all but killed me, and added a little aluminum ventilator to make sure of permanency in the form of the balloon.

This ventilator was a rotary fan, worked by the motor to send air into the little interior air balloon, which was sewed inside to the

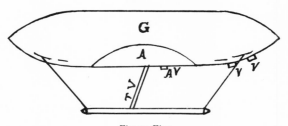

Figure Five

bottom of the great balloon like a kind of closed pocket. In Figure 5, *G* is the great balloon filled with hydrogen gas; *A*, the interior air balloon; *VV*, the automatic gas valves; *AV*, the air valve; and *TV*, the tube by which the rotary ventilator fed the interior air balloon.

The air valve, *AV*, was an exhaust valve similar to the two gas valves, *VV*, in the great balloon, with the one exception that it was weaker. In this way, when there happened to be too much fluid (*i.e.,* gas or air, or both) distending the great balloon, all the air would leave the interior balloon before any of the gas would leave the great balloon.

The first trial of my "No. 2" was set for May 11, 1899. Unfortunately the weather, which had been fine in the morning, grew steadily rainy in the afternoon. In those days I had no balloon house of my own. All the morning the balloon had been slowly filling with hydrogen gas at the captive balloon station of the Jardin d'Acclimatation. As there was no shed there for me, the work had to be done in the open, and it was done vexatiously, with a hundred delays, surprises, and excuses.

When the rain came on, it wetted the balloon. What was to be done? I must either empty it and lose the hydrogen and all my time and trouble, or go on under the disadvantage of a rain-soaked balloon envelop heavier than it ought to be.

I chose to go up in the rain. No sooner had I risen than the weather caused a great contraction of the hydrogen so that the long, cylindrical balloon shrunk visibly. Then before the air pump could remedy the fault, a strong wind gust of the rainstorm doubled it up worse than the "No. 1," and tossed it into the neighboring trees.

My friends began at me again, saying:

"This time you have learned your lesson. You must understand that it is impossible to keep the shape of your cylindrical balloon rigid. You must not again risk your life by taking a petroleum motor up beneath it."

I said to myself:

"What has the rigidity of the balloon's form to do with danger from a petroleum motor? Errors do not count. I have learned my lesson, but it is not that lesson."

Accordingly, I immediately set to work on a "No. 3," with a shorter and very much thicker balloon, 20 meters (66 feet) long and 7.5 meters (25 feet) at its greatest diameter. (Figure 6.) Its much greater gas capacity — 500 cubic meters (17,650 cubic feet) — would give it, with hydrogen, three times the lifting power of my first and twice that of my second airship. This permitted me to use common illuminating gas, whose lifting power is about half that of hydrogen. The hydrogen plant of the Jardin d'Acclimatation had always served me badly. With illuminating gas I should be free to start from the establishment of my balloon constructor or elsewhere, as I desired.

11. Accident to the "Santos-Dumont No. 2," May 11, 1899 (first phase)

12. Accident to the "Santos-Dumont No. 2," May 11, 1899 (second phase)

It will be seen that I was getting far away from the cylindrical shapes of my first two balloons. In the future I told myself that I would at least avoid doubling up. The rounder form of this balloon also made it possible to dispense with the interior air balloon and its feeding air pump that had twice refused to work adequately at the critical moment. Should this shorter and thicker balloon need aid to keep its form rigid, I relied on the stiffening effect of a 33-foot bamboo pole (see Figure 6) fixed lengthwise to the suspension cords above my head and directly beneath the balloon.

While not yet a true keel, this pole keel supported basket and guide rope and brought my shifting weights into much more effectual play.

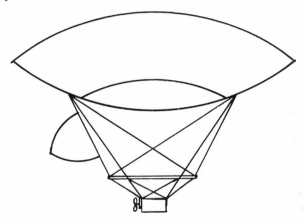

Figure Six

On November 13, 1899, I started in the "Santos-Dumont No. 3," from the establishment of Vaugirard, on the most successful flight that I had yet made.

From Vaugirard I went directly to the Champ de Mars, which I had chosen for its clear, open space. There I was able to practice aerial navigation to my heart's content, circling, driving ahead in straight courses, forcing the airship diagonally onward and upward and shooting diagonally downward by propeller force, and thus acquiring mastery of my shifting weights. These, because of the greater distance they were now set apart at the extremities of the pole keel (see Figure 6), worked with an effectiveness that astonished even myself. This proved my greatest triumph, for it was already clear to me that the central truth of dirigible ballooning must be ever — "To descend without sacrificing gas and to mount without sacrificing ballast."

During these first evolutions over the Champ de Mars, I had no particular thought of the Eiffel Tower. At most, it seemed a monument worth going round, and so I circled round it at a prudent distance again and again. Then — still without any dream of what the future had in store for me — I made a straight course for the Parc des Princes, over almost the exact line that, two years later, was to mark the Deutsch Prize route.

I steered to the Parc des Princes because it was another fine open space. Once there, however, I was loath to descend: so, making a hook, I navigated to the maneuver grounds of Bagatelle, where I finally landed in souvenir of my fall of the year previous. It was almost at the exact spot where the kite-flying boys had pulled on my guide rope and saved me from a bad shaking-up. At this time, remember, neither the Aéro Club nor I possessed a balloon park or shed from which to start and to which to return.

On this trip I considered that, had the air been calm, my speed in relation to the ground would have been as much as 25 kilometers (15 miles) per hour. In other words, I went at that rate through the air, the wind being strong though not violent. Therefore, even had not sentimental reasons led me to land at Bagatelle, I should have hesitated to return *with the wind* to the Vaugirard balloon house, itself of small size and difficult access, and surrounded by all the houses of a busy quarter. Landing in Paris, in general, is dangerous for any kind of balloon, amid chimney pots that threaten to pierce its belly and tiles that are always ready to be knocked down on the heads of passersby. When, in the future, airships become as common as automobiles are at present, spacious public and private landing stages will have to be built for them in every part of the capital. Already they have been foretold by Mr. Wells in his strange book *When the Sleeper Wakes.*

Considerations of this order made it desirable for me to have a plant of my own. I needed a building for the housing of my airship between trips. Heretofore I had emptied the balloon of all its gas at the end of each trip, as one is bound to do with spherical balloons. Now I saw very different possibilities for dirigibles. The significant thing was the fact that my "No. 3" had lost so little gas (or, perhaps, none at all) at the end of its first long trip that I could

13. Accident to the "Santos-Dumont No. 2," May 11, 1899 (third phase)

14.   The "Santos-Dumont No. 3"

well have housed it overnight and gone out again in it the next day!

I had no longer the slightest doubt of the success of my invention. I foresaw that I was going into airship construction as a sort of lifework. I should need my own workshop, my own balloon house, hydrogen plant, and connection with the illuminating gas mains.

The Aéro Club had just acquired some land on the newly opened Côteaux de Longchamps at Saint Cloud, and I concluded to build on it a great shed, long and high enough to house my airship with its balloon fully inflated, and furnished with all the facilities mentioned.

This aerodrome, which I built at my own expense, was 100 feet long, 23 feet wide, and 36 feet high. Even here I had to contend with the conceit and prejudice of artisans, which had already given me so much trouble at the Jardin d'Acclimatation. It was declared that the sliding doors of my aerodrome could not be made to slide on account of their great size. I had to insist. "Follow my directions," I said, "and do not concern yourselves with their practicability!" Although the men had named their own pay, it was a long time before I could get the better of this vainglorious stubbornness of theirs. When finished, the doors worked — naturally. Three years later the aerodrome built for me by the Prince of Monaco on my plans had still greater sliding doors.

While this first of my balloon houses was under construction, I made a number of other successful trips in the "No. 3," the last time losing my rudder and luckily landing on the plain at Ivry. I did not repair the "No. 3." Its balloon was too clumsy in form and its motor was too weak. I had now my own aerodrome and gas plant. I would build a new airship, and with it I should be able to experiment for longer periods and with more method.

CHAPTER XI

THE EXPOSITION SUMMER

The Exposition of 1900, with its learned congresses, was now approaching. Its International Congress of Aeronautics being set for the month of September, I resolved that the new airship should be ready to be shown to it.

This was my "No. 4," finished August 1, 1900, and by far the most familiar to the world at large of all my airships. This is due to the fact that when I won the Deutsch Prize, nearly eighteen months later and in quite a different construction, the newspapers of the world came out with old cuts of this "No. 4" which they had kept on file.

It was the airship with the bicycle saddle. In it the 33-foot bamboo pole of my "No. 3" came nearer to being a real keel in that it no longer hung above my head, but — amplified by vertical and horizontal crosspieces and a system of tightly stretched cords — it sustained within itself motor, propeller, and connecting machinery, petroleum reservoir, ballast, and navigator, in a kind of spider web without a basket.

I was obliged to sit in the midst of the spider web below the balloon on the saddle of a bicycle frame which I had incorporated into it. Thus the absence of the traditional balloon basket appeared to leave me astride a pole in the midst of a confusion of ropes, tubes, and machinery. Nevertheless the device was very handy, because round this bicycle frame I had united cords for controlling the shifting weights, for striking the motor's electric spark, for opening and shutting the balloon's valves, for turning on and off the water ballast spigots, and for certain other functions of the airship. Under my feet I had the starting pedals of a new 7 horsepower petroleum motor driving a propeller with two wings, each 4 meters (13 feet) across. They were of silk stretched over steel plates and very strong. For steering, my hands reposed on the bicycle handlebars connected with my rudder.

Above all this there stretched the balloon, 39 meters (129 feet) long, with a middle diameter of 5.1 meters (17 feet) and a gas capacity of 420 cubic meters (nearly 15,000 cubic feet). In form it was a compromise between the slender cylinders of my first constructions and the clumsy compactness of my "No. 3." (See Figure 7.) For this reason I thought it prudent to give it an interior compensating air balloon fed by a rotary ventilator like that of the "No. 2"; and as the balloon was smaller than its predecessor, I was obliged to return again to hydrogen to get sufficient lifting power. For

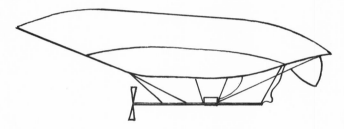

Figure Seven

that matter, there was no longer any reason why I should not employ hydrogen. I now had my own hydrogen gas generator, and my "No. 4," safely housed in the aerodrome, might be kept inflated during weeks.

In the "Santos-Dumont No. 4" I also tried the experiment of placing the propeller at the stem instead of the stern of the airship. So, attached to the pole keel in front, the screw pulled instead of pushing it through the air. The new 7 horsepower motor with two cylinders turned it with a velocity of 100 revolutions per minute, and produced, from a fixed point, a traction-effort of some 30 kilograms (66 pounds).

The pole keel with its cross pieces, bicycle frame, and mechanism weighed heavy. Therefore, although the balloon was filled with hydrogen, I could not take up more than 50 kilograms (110 pounds) of ballast.

I made almost daily experiments with this new airship during

August and September, 1900, at the Aéro Club's grounds at Saint Cloud, but my most memorable trial with it took place on September 19, in presence of the members of the International Congress of Aeronautics. Although an accident to my rudder at the last moment prevented me from making a free ascent before these men of science, I nevertheless held my own against a very strong wind that was blowing at the time, and gave what they were good enough to proclaim a satisfying demonstration of the effectiveness of an aerial propeller driven by a petroleum motor. A distinguished member of the congress, Professor Langley, desired to be present a few days later at one of my usual trials, and from him I received the heartiest kind of encouragement.

The result of these trials was, nevertheless, to decide me to double the propeller's power by the adoption of the four cylinder type of petroleum motor without water jacket; that is to say, the system of cooling *à ailettes*. The new motor was delivered to me very promptly; and I immediately set about adapting the airship to it. Its extra weight demanded either that I should construct a new balloon or else enlarge the old one. I tried the latter course. Cutting the balloon in half, I had a piece put in it, as one puts a leaf in an extension table. This brought the balloon's length to 33 meters (109 feet). Then I found that the aerodrome was too short by 10 feet to receive it! In provision for future needs, I added 4 meters (13 feet) to its length.

Motor, balloon, and shed were all transformed in fifteen days. The Exposition was still open, but the autumn rains had set in. After waiting with the balloon filled with hydrogen through two weeks of the worst possible weather, I let out the gas and began experimenting with the motor and propeller. It was not lost time, for, bringing the speed of the propeller up to 140 revolutions per minute, I realized, from a fixed point, a traction effort of 55 kilograms (120 pounds). Indeed, the propeller turned with such force that I was stricken with pneumonia in its current of cold air.

I betook myself to Nice for the pneumonia, and there, while convalescing, an idea came to me. This new idea took the form of my first true airship keel.

In a small carpenter shop at Nice I worked it out with my own hands — a long, triangular-sectioned pine framework of great lightness and rigidity. Though 18 meters (59½ feet) in length, it weighed only 41 kilograms (90 pounds). Its joints were of aluminum; and,

15. Professor Langley visits the "Santos-Dumont No. 4"

16. Motor of the "Santos-Dumont No. 4"

to secure its lightness and rigidity, to cause it to offer less resistance to the air, and to make it less subject to hygrometric variations, it occurred to me to reinforce it with tightly drawn piano wires instead of cords.

Then followed what turned out to be an entirely new idea in aeronautics. I asked myself why I should not use this same piano wire for all my dirigible balloon suspensions in place of the cords and ropes used in all kinds of balloons up to this time. I did it; and the innovation turned out to be peculiarly valuable. These piano wires, 0.032 inch in diameter, possess a high coefficient of rupture and a surface so slight that their substitution for the ordinary cord suspensions constitutes a greater progress than many a more showy device. Indeed, it has been calculated that the cord suspensions offered almost as much resistance to the air as did the balloon itself!

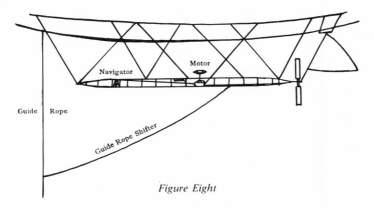

Figure Eight

At the stern of this airship keel I again established my propeller. I had found no advantage result from placing it in front on my "No. 4," where it was an actual hindrance to the free working of the guide rope. The propeller was now driven by a new 12 horsepower four cylinder motor without water jacket, through the intermediary of a long, hollow steel shaft. Placing this motor in the center of the keel (*Motor,* Figure 8), I balanced its weight by taking my position in my basket well to the front (*Navigator,* Figure 8) while the guide rope hung suspended from a point still farther forward (*Guide Rope,* Figure 8). To it, some distance down its length, I fastened the end of a lighter cord run up to a pulley fixed in the afterpart of the keel and thence to my basket, where I fastened it convenient

to my hand (*Guide Rope Shifter,* Figure 8). Thus I made the guide
rope do the work of shifting weights. Imagine, for example, that
going on a straight horizontal course, as in Figure 8, I should decide
to rise. I would have but to pull in the guide rope shifter. It would
pull the guide rope itself back (Figure 9), and thus shift back the
center of gravity of the whole system that much. The stem of the
airship would rise (as in Figure 9), and, consequently, my propeller
force would push me up along the new diagonal line.

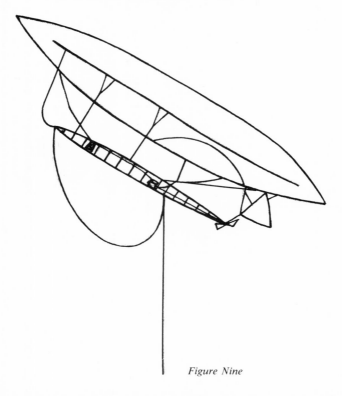

Figure Nine

The rudder was fixed at the stern, as usual, and water ballast cylinders, accessory shifting weights, petroleum reservoir, and the other
parts of the machinery were disposed in the new keel, well balanced.
For the first time in these experiments — as well as the first time
in aeronautics — I used liquid ballast. Two brass reservoirs, very
thin and holding altogether twelve gallons, were filled with water

and fixed in the keel, as above stated, between motor and propeller, and their two spigots were so arranged that they could be opened and shut from my basket by means of two steel wires.

Before this new keel was fitted to the enlarged balloon of my "No. 5," and in acknowledgment of the work I had done in 1900, the Scientific Commission of the Paris Aéro Club had awarded me its Encouragement Prize, founded by M. Deutsch (de la Meurthe), and consisting of the yearly interest on one hundred thousand francs. To induce others to follow up the difficult and expensive problem of dirigible ballooning, I left this four thousand francs at the disposition of the Aéro Club to found a new prize. I made the conditions of winning it very simple:

> The Santos-Dumont Prize shall be awarded to the aeronaut, a member of the Paris Aéro Club and not the founder of this prize, who, between May 1 and October 1, 1901, starting from the Parc d'Aérostation of Saint Cloud, shall turn around the Eiffel Tower and come back to the starting-point, at the end of whatever time, without having touched ground and by his self-contained means on board alone.
>
> If the Santos-Dumont Prize is not won in 1901, it shall remain open the following year, always from May 1 to October 1, and so on until it be won.

The Aéro Club signified the importance of such a trial by deciding to give its highest reward — a gold medal — to the winner of the Santos-Dumont Prize, as may be seen by its minutes of the time. Since then the four thousand francs have remained in the treasury of the Club.

CHAPTER XII

THE DEUTSCH PRIZE AND ITS PROBLEMS

This brings me to the Deutsch Prize for aerial navigation, offered in the spring of 1900 while I was navigating my "No. 3," and after I had, on at least one occasion — all unknowing — steered over what was to be its exact course from the Eiffel Tower to the Seine at Bagatelle.

This prize of one hundred thousand francs, founded by M. Deutsch (de la Meurthe), a member of the Paris Aéro Club, was to be awarded by the Scientific Commission of that organization to the first dirigible balloon or airship that, between May 1 and October 1, 1900, 1901, 1902, 1903, and 1904, should rise from the Parc d'Aérostation of the Aéro Club at Saint Cloud and, without touching ground and by its own self-contained means on board alone, describe a closed curve in such a way that the axis of the Eiffel Tower should be within the interior of the circuit, and return to the point of departure in the maximum time of half an hour. Should more than one accomplish the task in the same year, the one hundred thousand francs were to be divided in proportion to their respective times.

The Aéro Club's Scientific Commission had been named expressly for the purpose of formulating these and such other conditions of the foundation as it might deem proper, and by reason of certain of them I had made no attempt to win the prize with my "Santos-Dumont No. 4." The course from the Aéro Club's Parc d'Aérostation to the Eiffel Tower and return was nearly seven miles; and this distance *plus the turning around the tower* must be accomplished in thirty minutes. This meant in a perfect calm a necessary speed of fifteen and a half miles per hour for the straight stretches — a speed I could not be sure to maintain all the way in my "No. 4."

Another condition formulated by the Scientific Commission was that its members — who were to be judges of all trials — must be notified twenty-four hours in advance of each attempt. Naturally the operation of such a condition would be to nullify as much as possible all minute time calculations based either on a given rate of speed through perfect calm or such air current as might be prevailing twenty-four hours previous to the hour of trial. Though Paris is situated in a basin, surrounded on all sides by hills, its air currents are peculiarly variable; and brusque meteorological changes are extremely common.

I foresaw, also, that when a competitor had once committed the formal act of assembling a scientific commission on a slope of the River Seine so far away from Paris as Saint Cloud, he would be under a kind of moral pressure to go on with his trial, no matter how the air currents might have increased, and no matter in what kind of weather — wet, dry, or simply humid — he might find himself.

Again, this moral pressure to go on with the trial against the aeronaut's better judgment must extend even to the event of an unlucky change in the state of the airship itself. One does not convoke a body of prominent personages to a distant riverside for nothing; yet in the twenty-four hours between notification and trial even a well-watched elongated balloon might well lose a little of its tautness unperceived. A previous day's preliminary trial might easily derange so uncertain an engine as the petroleum motor of the year 1900. And, finally, I saw that the competitor would be barred by common courtesy from convoking the commission at the very hour most favorable for dirigible balloon experiments over Paris — the calm of the dawn. The duelist may call out his friends at that sacred hour, but not the airship captain!

In founding the Santos-Dumont Prize with the four thousand francs awarded to me by the Aéro Club for my work in the year 1900, it will be observed that I made no such conditions by the way. I did not wish to complicate the trial by imposing a minimum velocity, the check of a special committee, or any limitation of time of trial during the day. I was sure that even under the widest conditions it would be a great deal to come back to the starting-point after having reached a post publicly pointed out in advance — a thing that was unheard of before the year 1901.

The conditions of the Santos-Dumont Prize, therefore, left competitors free to choose the state of the air least unfavorable to them, as the calm of late evening or early morning. Nor would I inflict on them the possible surprises of a period of waiting between the convocation and the meeting of a scientific commission, itself, in my eyes, quite unnecessary in these days when the army of newspaper reporters of a great capital is always ready to mobilize without notice, at any hour and spot, on the bare prospect of news. The newspaper men of Paris would be my scientific commission.

As I had excluded myself from trying for the Santos-Dumont Prize, I naturally wished to show that it would not be impossible to fulfil its conditions. My "No. 5" — composed of the enlarged balloon of the "No. 4" and the new keel, motor, and propeller already described — was now ready for trial. In it, on the first attempt, I fulfilled the conditions of my own prize foundation.

This was on July 12, 1901, after a practice flight the day before. At 4:30 A.M. I steered my airship from the park of the Aéro Club at Saint Cloud to the Longchamps racecourse. I did not at that moment take time to ask permission of the Jockey Club, which, however, a few days later, placed that admirable open space at my disposition. Ten times in succession I made the circuit of Longchamps, stopping each time at a point designed beforehand.

After these first evolutions, which altogether made up a distance of about 35 kilometers (22 miles), I set out for Puteaux, and after an excursion of about 3 kilometers (2 miles), done in nine minutes, I steered back again to Longchamps.

I was by this time so well satisfied with the dirigibility of my "No. 5" that I began looking for the Eiffel Tower. It had disappeared in the mists of the morning, but its direction was well known to me, so I steered for it as well as I might.

In ten minutes I had come within 200 meters (40 rods) of the Champ de Mars. At this moment one of the cords managing my rudder broke. It was absolutely necessary to repair it at once, and to repair it, I must descend to earth. With perfect ease I pulled forward the guide rope, shifted my center of gravity, and drove the airship diagonally downward, landing gently in the Trocadéro Gardens. Good-natured workmen ran to me from all directions.

Did I need anything? they asked.

Yes, I needed a ladder. And in less time than it takes to write it, a ladder was found and placed in position. While two of these dis-

17. The "Santos-Dumont No. 5"

18. The "Santos-Dumont No. 5" landing at the Trocadéro for repairs

creet and intelligent volunteers held it, I climbed some twenty rounds to its top and was able to repair the damaged rudder connection.

I started off again, mounting diagonally to my chosen altitude, turned the Eiffel Tower in a wide curve, and returned to Long-champs in a straight course without further incident after a trip, including the stop for repairs, of one hour and six minutes. Then, after a few minutes' conversation, I took my flight back to the Saint Cloud aerodrome, passing the Seine at an altitude of 200 meters (over 600 feet), and housing the still perfectly inflated airship in its shed as though it were a simple automobile.

CHAPTER XIII

A FALL BEFORE A RISE

My "No. 5" had proved itself so much more powerful than its predecessors that I now found courage to inscribe myself for the Deutsch Prize competition.

Having taken this decisive step, I at once convoked the Scientific Commission of the Aéro Club for a trial, in accordance with the regulations.

The commission assembled in the grounds of the Aéro Club at Saint Cloud on July 13, 1901, at 6:30 A.M. At 6:41 I started off. I turned the Eiffel Tower in the tenth minute, and came back against an unexpected headwind, reaching the time-keepers at Saint Cloud in the fortieth minute, at an altitude of 200 meters and after a terrific struggle with the element.

Just at this moment my capricious motor stopped, and the airship, bereft of its power, drifted until it fell on the tallest chestnut tree in the park of M. Edmond de Rothschild. The inhabitants and servants of the villa, who came running, very naturally imagined that the airship must be wrecked and myself probably hurt. They were astonished to find me standing in my basket high up in the tree, while the propeller touched the ground. Considering the force with which the wind had blown when I was battling with it on the home-stretch, I myself was surprised to note how little the balloon was torn. Nevertheless, all its gas had left it.

This happened very near the house of the Princess Isabel, Comtesse d'Eu, who, hearing of my plight, and learning that I must be occupied some time in disengaging the airship, sent a lunch to me up in my tree, with an invitation to come and tell her the story of my trip. When the story was finished, the daughter of Dom Pedro said to me:

19.   The "Santos-Dumont No. 5" over the Longchamps racecourse

20. Accident in the park of M. Edmond Rothschild

"Your evolutions in the air make me think of the flight of our great birds of Brazil. I hope that you will do as well with your propeller as they do with their wings, and that you will succeed for the glory of our common country!"

A few days later I received the following letter:

August 1, 1901

MONSIEUR SANTOS-DUMONT:

Here is a medal of St. Benedict that protects against accidents.

Accept it and wear it, at your watch chain, in your card case, or at your neck.

I send it to you, thinking of your good mother, and praying God to help you always and to make you work for the glory of our country.

ISABEL, Comtesse d'Eu

As the newspapers have often spoken of my "bracelet," I may say that the thin gold chain of which it consists is simply the means I have taken to wear this medal, which I prize.

The airship, as a whole, was damaged very little, considering the force of the wind and the nature of the accident. When it was ready to be taken out again I therefore thought it prudent to make several trials with it over the grassy lawn of the Longchamps racecourse. One of these trials I will mention, because it gave me — something rare — a fairly accurate idea of the airship's speed in perfect calm. On this occasion Mr. Maurice Farman followed me around the racecourse in his automobile, at its second speed. His estimate was between 26 and 30 kilometers (16 and 18½ miles) per hour, with my guide rope dragging. Of course, when the guide rope drags, it acts exactly like a brake. How much it holds one back depends upon the length that actually drags along the ground. Our calculation at the time was about 5 kilometers (3 miles) per hour, which would have brought my proper speed up to between 30 and 35 kilometers (18½ and 21½ miles) per hour. All this encouraged me to make another trial for the Deutsch Prize.

And now I come to a terrible day — August 8, 1901. At 6:30 A.M., in presence of the Scientific Commission of the Aéro Club, I started again for the Eiffel Tower.

I turned the Tower at the end of nine minutes and took my way back to Saint Cloud, but my balloon was losing hydrogen through one of its two automatic gas valves, whose spring had been accidentally weakened.

I had perceived the beginning of this loss of gas even before reaching the Eiffel Tower, and ordinarily, in such an event, I should have come at once to earth to examine the lesion. But here I was competing for a prize of great honor and my speed had been good. Therefore I risked going on.

The balloon shrank visibly. By the time I had reached the fortifications of Paris near La Muette, it caused the suspension wires to sag so much that those nearest to the screw propeller caught in it as it revolved.

I saw the propeller cutting and tearing at the wires. I stopped the motor instantly. Then, as a consequence, the airship was at once driven back toward the Tower by the wind, which was strong.

At the same time I was falling. The balloon had lost much gas. I might have thrown out ballast and greatly diminished the fall, but then the wind would have time to blow me back on the Eiffel Tower. I therefore preferred to let the airship go down as it was going. It may have seemed a terrific fall to those who watched it from the ground, but to me the worst detail was the airship's lack of equilibrium. The half-empty balloon, fluttering its empty end as an elephant waves his trunk, caused the airship's stem to point upward at an alarming angle. What I most feared, therefore, was that the unequal strain on the suspension wires would break them one by one and so precipitate me to the ground.

Why was the balloon fluttering an empty end and causing all this extra danger? How was it that the rotary ventilator was not fulfilling its purpose in feeding the interior air balloon and in this manner swelling out the gas balloon around it? The answer must be looked for in the nature of the accident. The rotary ventilator stopped working when the motor itself stopped, and I had been obliged to stop the motor to prevent it from tearing the suspension wires near it when the balloon first began to sag from loss of gas. It is true that the ventilator, which was working at that moment, had not proved sufficient to prevent the first sagging. It may have been that the interior air balloon refused to fill out properly. The day after the accident, when my balloon constructor's man came to me for the plans of a "No. 6" balloon envelop, I gathered from something he said that the interior air balloon of the "No. 5," not having been given time for its varnish to dry before being adjusted, might have stuck together or stuck to the sides or bottom of the outer balloon. Such are the rewards of haste!

I was falling. At the same time the wind was carrying me toward the Eiffel Tower. It had already carried me so far that I was expecting to land on the Seine embankment beyond the Trocadéro. My basket and the whole of the keel had already passed the Trocadéro hotels, and, had my balloon been a spherical one, it too would have cleared the buildings. But now, at the last critical moment, the end of the long balloon that was still full of gas came slapping down on the roof just before clearing it! It exploded with a great noise — exactly like a paper bag struck after being blown up. This was the "terrific explosion" described in the newspapers of the day.

I had made a mistake in my estimate of the wind's force, by a few yards. Instead of being carried on to fall on the Seine embankment, I now found myself hanging in my wicker basket high up in the courtyard of the Trocadéro hotels, supported by my airship's keel, that stood braced at an angle of about forty-five degrees between the courtyard wall above and the roof of a lower construction farther down. The keel, in spite of my weight, that of the motor and machinery, and the shock it had received in falling, resisted wonderfully. The thin pine scantlings and piano wires of Nice had saved my life!

After what seemed tedious waiting, I saw a rope being lowered to me from the roof above. I held to it and was hauled up, when I perceived my rescuers to be the brave firemen of Paris. From their station at Passy they had been watching the flight of the airship. They had seen my fall and immediately hastened to the spot. Then, having rescued me, they proceeded to rescue the airship.

The operation was painful. The remains of the balloon envelop and the suspension wires hung lamentably, and it was impossible to disengage them except in strips and fragments!

So I escaped, and my escape may have been narrow. But it was not from the particular danger always present in my mind during this period of trials around the Eiffel Tower. A Parisian journalist said that, had the Eiffel Tower not existed, it would have been necessary to invent it for the needs of aerostation. It is true that the engineers who remain at its summit have at their hands all necessary instruments for observing aerial and meteorological conditions; their chronometers are exact; and, as Professor Langley has said in a communication to the Louisiana Purchase Exposition Committee, the position of the Tower as a central landmark, visible to every one from considerable distances, made it a unique winning post for an aerial contest. I myself had circled around it at a respectful distance, of my own free will, in 1899, before the stipulation of the Deutsch Prize competition was dreamed of. Yet none of these considerations altered the other fact that the necessity to round the Eiffel Tower attached a unique element of danger to the task.

What I feared was that, in my eagerness to make a quick turning, by some error in steering, or by the influence of some unexpected sidewind, I might be dashed against the Tower. The impact would certainly burst my balloon, and I should fall to the ground like a stone. Nor could the utmost prudence and self-control in making a wide turn guarantee me against the danger. Should my capricious motor stop as I approached the Tower — exactly as it stopped after I had passed over the timekeepers' heads at Saint Cloud returning from my first trial on July 13, 1901 — I would be powerless to hold the airship back.

Therefore I always dreaded the turn around the Eiffel Tower, looking on it as my principal danger. While never seeking to go high in my airships — on the contrary, I hold the record for low altitude in a free balloon — in passing over Paris I must necessarily move above and out of the way of its chimney pots and steeples. The Eiffel Tower was my one danger; yet it was my winning post!

Such were my fears while on the ground; while in the air I had no time for fear. I have always kept a cool head. Alone in the airship, I am always busy, for there is more than enough work for one man. Like the captain of a yacht, I must not let go the rudder for an instant. Like its chief engineer, I must watch the motor. The balloon's rigidity of form must be preserved. And with this capital detail is connected the whole complex problem of the airship's altitude, the maneuvering of guide rope and shifting weights, the economizing of ballast, and the surveillance of the air pump attached to the motor. Besides this, there is the joy of commanding rapid movement. The pleasurable sensations experienced in my first airships were intensified in the powerful "No. 5." As M. Jaurès has put it, I now felt myself a man in the air, commanding movement. In my spherical balloons I had felt myself to be only the shadow of a man!

21. Accident at the Trocadéro Hotel just before rescue by firemen

22. The "Santos-Dumont No. 6"

CHAPTER XIV

THE BUILDING OF MY "NO. 6"

On the very evening of my fall to the roof of the Trocadéro hotels, I gave out the specifications of a "Santos-Dumont No. 6"; and after twenty-two days of continuous labor, it was finished and inflated.

The new balloon had the shape of an elongated ellipsoid (Figure 10), 33 meters (110 feet) by its great axis and 6 meters (20 feet) by its small axis, terminated fore and aft by cones.

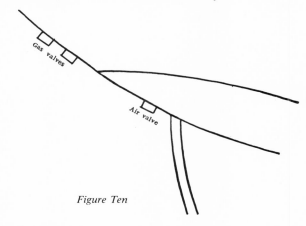

Figure Ten

I now gave greater care than ever to the devices on which I depended to maintain the balloon's rigidity of form. I had fallen to the roof of the Trocadéro hotels by the fault of the smallest and most insignificant looking piece of mechanism of the entire system — a weakened valve that let out the balloon's hydrogen. In very much the same way the fall of the first of all my airships had been occasioned by the failure of a little air pump!

In all my constructions, except the big-bellied balloon of the "No. 3," I had depended much on the interior compensating air balloon (Figure 5, page 49) fed by air pump or rotary ventilator. Sewed like a closed patch pocket to the bottom of the great balloon inside it, this compensating air balloon would remain flat and empty so long as the great balloon remained distended with its gas. Then, as hydrogen might be condensed from time to time by changes of altitude and temperature, the air pump or ventilator worked by the motor would begin to fill the compensating air balloon, make it take up more room inside the great balloon, and so keep it distended.

Inside the balloon of my "No. 6" I now sewed such a compensating balloon capable of holding 60 cubic meters (2118 cubic feet). The ventilator that was to feed it formed practically a part of the motor itself. In constant revolution while the motor worked, it would serve air continuously to the compensating balloon, whether or not the latter would be able to hold it. What air it could not hold would escape through a comparatively weak valve (*Air Valve,* Figure 10) communicating with the outer atmosphere through the bottom of the air balloon — which was also the bottom of the great outer balloon.

To relieve the great balloon of its dilated hydrogen when necessary, I supplied it with two of the best valves I could make. (*Gas Valves*, Figure 10.) These also communicated with the outer atmosphere. Imagine, now, that after a certain condensation of my hydrogen, the interior compensating balloon should have filled up in part with air from the ventilator and so maintained the form of the great balloon rigid. Shortly after, by a change of temperature or altitude, the hydrogen would begin to dilate again. Something would have to give way, or the balloon would burst in a "cold explosion." What ought to give way first? Evidently, the weaker air valve (*Air Valve,* Figure 10). Letting out part or all of the air in the interior balloon, it would relieve the tension of the swelling hydrogen. And only after, were this not sufficient, would the stronger gas valves (Figure 10) let out precious hydrogen.

All three valves were automatic, opening outward on a given pressure from within. One of the hypotheses to account for the terrible accident to the unhappy Severo's dirigible "Pax"[1] is con-

---

[1] In the early morning of May 12, 1902, M. August Severo, accompanied by his mechanic, Sachet, started from Paris on a first trial with the "Pax," the invention and construction of M. Severo. The "Pax" rose at once to a height almost double that of the Eiffel Tower, when, for reasons not precisely known, it exploded and came crashing to earth with its two passengers. The fall took eight seconds to accomplish, and the luckless experimenters were picked up broken and shapeless masses.

23. Accident to the "Santos-Dumont No. 6"

24. Motor of the "Santos-Dumont No. 6"

cerned with this all-important problem of valves. The "Pax," as originally constructed, had two. M. Severo, who was not a practical
aeronaut, stopped up one of them with wax before starting on his
first and last voyage. In view of the decreasing pressure of the atmosphere as one goes higher, the ascent of a dirigible should always be slow and never great, for gas will expand on the rise of a
few yards. It is quite different from the case of the spherical
balloon, which has no interior pressure to withstand. A dirigible,
whose envelop is distended by great pressure, depends on its valves
not to burst. With one of its valves stopped with wax, the "Pax"
was allowed to shoot up from the earth, and immediately its occu-
pants seem to have lost their heads. Instead of checking their rapid
rise, one of them threw out ballast — a handful of which will send
up a great spherical balloon perceptibly! The mechanic of Severo
is said to have been last seen throwing out a whole bag in his ex-
citement. Up shot the "Pax" higher and higher, and the expansion,
the explosion, and the awful fall came as a chain of consequences.

The tonnage of the new balloon was 630 cubic meters (22,239
cubic feet), affording an absolute lifting-power of 690 kilograms
(1518 pounds), but the increased weight of the new motor and machinery, nevertheless, put my disposable ballast at 110 kilograms
(242 pounds). It was a four-cylinder motor of 12 horsepower, cooled
automatically by the circulation of water round the top of the piston
(culasse). While the water cooler brought extra weight, I was glad
to have it, for the arrangement would permit me to utilize, without
fear of overheating or jamming en route, the full power of the motor,
which was able to communicate to the propeller a traction-effort
of 66 kilograms (145 pounds).

My daily practice with the new airship ended on September 6,
1901, in a slight accident. The balloon was reinflated by September
15, but four days later it crashed against a tree in making a too
sudden turn. Such accidents I have always taken philosophically,
looking on them as a kind of insurance against more terrible ones.
Were I to give a single word of caution to all dirigible balloonists,
it would be, "Keep close to earth!"

The place of the airship is not in high altitudes, and it is bétter to
catch in the tops of trees, as I used to do in the Bois de Boulogne,
than to risk the perils of the upper air without the slightest practical advantage!

CHAPTER XV

WINNING THE DEUTSCH PRIZE

And now, on October 19, 1901, the airship "Santos-Dumont No.
6" having been repaired with great celerity, I tried again for the
Deutsch Prize — and won it.

The day before, the weather had been wretched. Nevertheless, I
had sent out the necessary telegrams convoking the Commission.
Through the night the weather had improved, but the atmospheric
conditions at two o'clock in the afternoon — the hour announced for
the trial — were, nevertheless, so unfavorable that, of the twenty-
five members composing the Commission, only five made their appearance: MM. Deutsch (de la Meurthe), de Dion, Fonvielle, Be-
sançon, and Aimé.

The Central Meteorological Bureau, consulted at this hour by
telephone, reported a southeast wind blowing six meters per second
at the altitude of the Eiffel Tower. When I consider that I was content when my first airship, in 1898, had, in my opinion of myself and
friends, been going at the rate of seven meters per second, I am still
surprised at the progress realized in those three years, for I was now
setting out to win a race against a time limit in a wind blowing almost as fast as the highest speed I had realized in my first airship!

The official start took place at 2:42 P.M. In spite of the wind
striking me sidewise, with a tendency to take me to the left of the
Eiffel Tower, I held my course straight to that goal. Gradually I
drove the airship onward and upward to a height of about ten
meters above its summit. In doing this I lost some time, but secured
myself against accidental contact with the Tower as much as possible.

As I passed the Tower, I turned with a sudden movement of the

25. The "Santos-Dumont No. 6" leaving the balloon shed at the Aéro

26. Rounding the Eiffel Tower on the way to winning the Deutsch Prize

rudder, bringing the airship round the tower's lightning conductor at a distance of about fifty meters from it. The tower was thus turned at 2:51 P.M., the distance of 5½ kilometers *plus the turning,* being done in nine minutes.

The return trip was longer, being in the teeth of this same wind. Also, during the trip to the tower the motor had worked fairly well. Now, after I had left it some five hundred meters behind me, the motor was actually on the point of stopping! I had a moment of great uncertainty. I must make a quick decision. It was to abandon the steering wheel for a moment, at the risk of drifting from my course, in order to devote my attention to the carbureting lever and the lever controlling the electric spark.

The motor, which had almost stopped, began to work again. I had now reached the Bois, where, by a phenomenon known to all aeronauts, the cool air from the trees began making my balloon heavier and heavier — or, in true physics, smaller by condensation — all the time. By an unlucky coincidence, the motor at this moment began slowing again. Thus the airship was descending, while its motive power was decreasing!

To correct the descent, I had to throw back both guide rope and shifting weights. This caused the airship to point diagonally upward, so that what propeller force remained caused it to remount continually in the air.

I was now over the crowd of the Auteuil racetrack, already with a sharp pointing upward. I heard the applause of the mighty throng, when, suddenly, my capricious motor started working at full speed again. The suddenly accelerated propeller, being almost under the high-pointed airship, exaggerated the inclination, so that the applause of the crowd changed to cries of alarm. As for myself, I had no fear, being over the trees of the Bois, whose soft greenery, as I have already stated, always reassured me.

All this happened very quickly, before I had a chance to shift my weights and guide rope back to the normal horizontal positions. I was now at an altitude of one hundred and fifty meters. Of course I might have checked the diagonal mounting of the airship by the simple means of slowing the motor that was driving it upward, but I was racing against a time limit, and so I just went on.

I soon righted myself by shifting the guide rope and the weights forward. I mention this in detail because at the time many of my friends imagined something terrible was happening. All the same, I did not have time to bring the airship to a lower altitude before reaching the timekeepers in the Aéro Club's grounds — a thing I might easily have done by slowing the motor. This is why I passed so high over the judges' heads.

On my way to the Tower I never looked down on the housetops of Paris. I navigated in a sea of white and azure, seeing nothing but the goal. On the return trip I had kept my eyes fixed on the verdure of the Bois de Boulogne and the silver streak of river where I had to cross it. Now, at my high altitude of one hundred and fifty meters and with the propeller working at full power, I passed above Longchamps, crossed the Seine, and continued on at full speed over the heads of the Commission and the spectators gathered in the Aéro Club's grounds. At that moment it was eleven minutes and thirty seconds past three o'clock — making the time exactly twenty-nine minutes and thirty seconds.

The airship, carried by the impetus of its great speed, passed on, as a racehorse passes the winning post, as a sailing yacht passes the winning line, as a road racing automobile continues flying past the judges who have snapped its time. Like the jockey of the racehorse, I then turned and drove myself back to the aerodrome, to have my guide rope caught and be drawn down at twelve minutes forty and four-fifths seconds past three, or thirty minutes and forty-one seconds from the start.

I did not yet know my exact time.

I cried:

"Have I won?"

And the crowd of spectators cried back to me:

"Yes!"

For a while there were those who argued that my time ought to be calculated up to the moment of my second return to the aerodrome, instead of to the moment when I first passed over it returning from the Eiffel Tower. For a while, indeed, it seemed that it might be more difficult to have the prize awarded to me than it had been to win it. In the end, however, common sense prevailed. The money of the prize, amounting in all to 125,000 francs, I did not desire to keep. I therefore divided it into unequal parts. The greater sum, of 75,000 francs, I handed over to the Prefect of Police of Paris, to be used for the deserving poor. The balance I distributed among my employees, who had been so long with me and to whose devotion I was glad to pay this tribute.

27. Scientific commission of the Aéro Club observing the winning of the
Deutsch Prize

28. Medal awarded to Santos-Dumont by the Brazilian government

At this same time, I received another grand prize, as gratifying as it was unexpected. This was a sum of 100 contos (125,000 francs) voted to me by the government of my own country and accompanied by a gold medal of large size and great beauty, designed, engraved, and struck off in Brazil. Its obverse shows my humble self, led by Victory and crowned with laurel by a flying figure of Renown. Above a rising sun there is engraved the line of Camoëns, altered by one word, as I adopted it to float on the long streamer of my airship: *"Por* CEOS *nunca d'antes navegados!"[1]* The reverse bears these words: "Being President of the Republic of the United States of Brazil, the Doctor Manoel Ferraz de Campos Salles has given order to engrave and strike this medal in homage to Alberto Santos-Dumont, 19 October, 1901."

---

[1]"Through *heavens* heretofore unsailed" — instead of: *Por* MARES *nunca d'antes navegados* ("O'er *seas* heretofore unsailed").

CHAPTER XVI

A GLANCE BACKWARD AND
FORWARD

Just as I had not gone into airship constructing for the sake of winning the Deutsch Prize, so now I had no reason to stop experimenting after I had won it. When I built and navigated my first airships, neither Aéro Club nor Deutsch Prize was yet in existence. The two, by their rapid rise and deserved prominence, had brought the problem of aerial navigation suddenly before the public — so suddenly, indeed, that I was really not prepared to enter into such a race with a time limit. Naturally anxious to have the honor of winning such a competition, I had been forced on rapidly in new constructions at both danger and expense. Now I would take time to perfect myself systematically as an aerial navigator.

Suppose you buy a new bicycle or automobile. You will have a perfect machine in your hand, without having had any of the labor, the deceptions, the false starts and recommencements of the inventor and constructor. Yet with all these advantages you will soon find that possession of the perfected machine does not necessarily mean that you shall go spinning over the highways with it. You may be so unpracticed that you will fall off the bicycle or blow up the automobile. The machine is all right, but you must learn to run it.

To bring the modern bicycle to its perfection, thousands of amateurs, inventors, engineers, and constructors labored during more than twenty-five years, trying endless innovations, one by one rejecting the great mass of them and, after endless failures by the way of half successes, slowly nearing to the perfect organism.

So it is today with the automobile. Imagine the united labors and financial sacrifices of the engineers and manufacturers that led, step by step, up to the road racing automobiles of the Paris-Berlin Competition in 1901 — the year in which the only working dirigible balloon then in existence won the Deutsch Prize against a time limit that was thought by many a complete bar to success. Yet of the 170 perfected automobiles registered for entry in the Paris-Berlin Competition, only 109 completed the first day's run, and of these only 26 finally reached Berlin!

Out of 170 automobiles entered for the race, only 26 reached the goal! And of these 26 arriving at Berlin, how many do you imagine made the trip without serious accident? Perhaps none!

It is perfectly natural that this should be so. People think nothing of it. Such is the natural development of a great invention. But if I break down while in the air, I cannot stop for repairs; I must go on, and the whole world knows it!

Looking back, therefore, on my progress since the time I doubled up above the Bagatelle grounds in 1898, I was surprised at the rapid pace at which I had allowed the notice of the world and my own ardor to push me on in what was in reality an arbitrary task. At the risk of my neck and the needless sacrifice of a great deal of money, I had won the Deutsch Prize. I might have arrived at the same point of progress by less forced and more reasonable stages. Throughout I had been inventor, patron, manufacturer, amateur, mechanic, and airship captain, all united! Yet any one of these qualities is thought to bring sufficient work and credit to the individual in the world of automobiles.

With all these cares I often found myself criticized for choosing calm days for my experiments. Yet who, experimenting over Paris — as I had to do when trying for the Deutsch Prize — would add to his natural risks and expenses the vexations of who knows what prosecutions for knocking down the chimney pots of a great capital on the heads of a population of pedestrians?

One by one I tried the assurance companies. None would make a rate for me against the damage I might do on a squally day. None would give me a rate on my own airship to insure it against destruction.

To me it was now clear that what I most needed was navigation practice pure and simple. I had been increasing the speed of my airships — that is to say, I had been constructing — at the expense of my education as an airship captain.

The captain of a steamboat obtains his certificate only after years of study and experience of navigation in inferior capacities. Even the chauffeur on the public highway must pass his examination before the authorities will give him his papers.

In the air, where all is new, the routine navigation of a dirigible balloon, requiring for foundation the united experiences of the spherical balloonist and the automobile chauffeur, makes demands upon the lone captain's coolness, ingenuity, quick reasoning, and a kind of instinct that comes with long habit.

Urged on by these considerations, my great object in the autumn of 1901 was to find a favorable place for practice in aerial navigation.

My swiftest and best airship — "Santos-Dumont No. 6" — was in perfect condition. The day after winning the Deutsch Prize in it, my chief mechanic asked me if he should tighten it up with hydrogen. I told him yes. Then, seeking to let some more hydrogen into it, he discovered something curious. The balloon would not take any more! It had not lost a single cubic unit of hydrogen.

The winning of the Deutsch Prize had cost only a few liters of petroleum!

Just as the Paris winter of biting winds, cold rains, and lowering skies was approaching, I received an intimation that the Prince of Monaco, himself a man of science celebrated for his personal investigations, would be pleased to build a balloon house directly on the beach of La Condamine, from which I might dart out on the Mediterranean and so continue my aerial practice through the winter.

The situation promised to be ideal. The little Bay of Monaco, sheltered from behind against the wind and cold by mountains, and from the wind and sea on either side by the heights of Monte Carlo and Monaco town, would make a well-protected maneuver ground.

The airship would be always ready, filled with hydrogen gas. It could slip out of the balloon house to profit by good weather, and back again for shelter at the approach of squalls. The balloon house would be erected on the edge of the shore, and the whole Mediterranean would lie before me for guide-roping.

29.   In the Bay of Monaco

30. From Cap Martin to Monte Carlo

CHAPTER XVII

MONACO AND THE
MARITIME GUIDE ROPE

When I arrived at Monte Carlo, in the latter part of January, 1902, the balloon house of the Prince of Monaco was already practically completed, from suggestions I had given.

The new aerodrome rose on the Boulevard de la Condamine, just across the electric tramcar tracks from the seawall. It was an immense empty shell of wood and canvas over a stout iron skeleton 180 feet long, 33 feet wide, and 50 feet high. It had to be solidly constructed, not to invite the fate of the all-wood aerodrome of the French Maritime Ballooning Station at Toulon, twice wrecked and once all but carried away, like a veritable wooden balloon, by tempests!

In spite of the aerodrome's risky form and curious construction, its sensational features were its doors. Tourists told one another (quite correctly) that doors so great as these had never been before, in ancient times or modern. They had been made to slide open and shut, above on wheels hanging from an iron construction that extended from the façade on each side, and below on wheels that rolled over a rail. Each door was 50 feet high by 16½ feet wide, and each weighed 9680 pounds. Yet their equilibrium was so well calculated that on the day of the inauguration of the aerodrome, these giant doors were rolled apart by two little boys of eight and ten years respectively, the young Princes Ruspoli, grandsons of the Duc de Dino, my host at Monte Carlo.

While the new situation attracted me by its promise of convenient and protected winter practice, the prospect of doing some over sea navigation with my airship was even more alluring. Even to the spherical balloonist, the over sea problem has great temptations, concerning which an expert of the French navy has said:

"The balloon can render the navy immense services *on condition that its direction can be assured.*

"Floating over the sea, it can be at once scout and offensive auxiliary of so delicate a character that the General Service of the navy has not yet allowed itself to pronounce on the matter. We can no longer conceal it from ourselves, however, that the hour approaches when balloons, becoming new military engines, will acquire from the point of view of battle results a great and perhaps decisive *action de guerre.*"

As for myself, I have never made it any secret that, to my mind, the first practical use of the airship will be found in war, and the farseeing Henri Rochefort, who was in the habit of coming to the aerodrome from his hotel at La Turbie, wrote a most significant editorial in this sense after I had laid before him the speed calculations of my "No. 7," then in course of building.

"The day when it shall be established that a man can make his airship travel in a given direction and maneuver it at will during the four hours which the young Santos demands to go from Monaco to Calvi," wrote Henri Rochefort, "there will remain little more for the nations to do than to throw down their arms. . . .

"I am astonished that the capital importance of this matter has not yet been grasped by all the professionals of aerostation. To mount in a balloon that one has not constructed and which one is not in a state to guide constitutes the easiest of performances. A little cat has done it at the Folies-Bergère. . . ."

Now, in war service over land the airship will, doubtless, often have to mount to considerable heights to avoid the rifle fire of the enemy, but as the maritime auxiliary described by the expert of the French navy, its scouting role will, for the most part, be performed at the end of its guide rope comparatively close to the waves and yet high enough to take in a wide view. Only when, for easily imagined reasons, it is desired to mount high for a short time will it quit the convenient contact of its guide rope with the surface of the sea.

For these considerations — and particularly the last — I was anxious to do a great deal of guide roping over the Mediterranean. If the maritime experiment promises so much to spherical ballooning, it is doubly promising to the airship which, from the nature of its construction, carries comparatively little ballast. This ballast ought not to be currently sacrificed, as it is by the spherical balloonist, for the remedying of every little vertical aberration. Its purpose is for use in great emergencies. Nor ought the aerial navigator, particularly if he be alone, be forced to rectify his altitude continually by means of his propeller and shifting weights. He ought to be free to navigate his airship; if on pleasure bent, with ease and leisure to enjoy his flight; if on war service, with facility for his observations and hostile maneuvers. Therefore any *automatic* guarantee of vertical stability is peculiarly welcome to him.

You know already what the guide rope is. I have described it in my first experience of spherical ballooning. Over land, where there are level plains or roads, or even streets, where there are not too

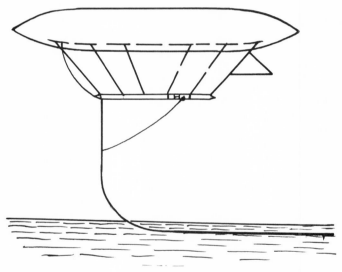

Figure Eleven

many troublesome trees, buildings, fences, telegraph and trolley poles and wires and like irregularities, the guide rope is as great an aid to the airship as to the spherical balloon. Indeed, I have made it more so, for with me it is the central feature of my shifting-weights (Figures 8 and 9).

Over the uninterrupted stretches of the sea, my first Monaco flight proved it to be a true *stabilisateur*. Its very slight dragging resistance through the water is out of all proportion to the considerable weight of its floating extremity. According to its greater or less immersion, therefore, it ballasts or unballasts the airship (Figure 11). The balloon is held by the weight of the guide rope down to a fixed level over the waves, without danger of being drawn into contact with them. For the moment that the airship descends the slightest distance nearer to them, that very moment it becomes relieved of just so much weight, and must naturally rise again by that amount of momentary unballasting. In this way an incessant little tugging toward and away from the waves is produced, infinitely gentle, an automatic ballasting and unballasting of the airship without loss of ballast!

My first flight over the Mediterranean, which was made on the morning of January 29, 1902, proved more than this, unfortunately. It was seen that a miscalculation had been made with respect to the site of the aerodrome itself. In the navigation of the air, where all is new, such surprises meet the experimenter at every turn. This ought to be remembered when one takes account of progress. In the Paris-Madrid automobile race of 1903 what minute precautions were not taken to secure the competitors against the perils of quick turnings and grade crossings! And yet how notably insufficient did they not turn out to be!

As the airship was being taken out from its house for its first flight on the morning of January 29, 1902, the spectators could see that nothing equivalent to the landing stages which the airships of the future must have built for them existed in front of the building. The airship, loaded with ballast until it was a trifle heavier than the surrounding atmosphere, had to be towed or helped out of the aerodrome and across the Boulevard de la Condamine before it could be launched into the air over the seawall.

Now that seawall proved to be a dangerous obstruction. From the sidewalk it was only waist high, but on the other side of it the surf rolled over pebbles from four to five meters below.

The airship had to be lifted over the seawall more than waist high, also, not to risk damaging the arms of its propeller, and when half over, there was no one to sustain it from the other side. Its stem pointed obliquely downward, while its stern threatened to grind on the wall. Scuffling among the pebbles below, on the sea side, half a dozen workmen held their arms high toward the descending keel as it was let down and pushed on toward them by the workmen in charge of it on the boulevard in front of the wall, and they were at last able to catch and right it only in time to prevent me from being precipitated from the basket.

For this reason my return to the aerodrome after this first flight

31. The balloon house at La Condamine

32.   Interior of the balloon shed, Monte Carlo

became the occasion of a real triumph for the crowd promptly took cognizance of the perils of the situation and foresaw difficulties for me when I should attempt to reenter the balloon house. As there was no wind, however, and as I steered boldly, I was able to make a sensational entry without damage — and without aid! Straight as a dart the airship sped to the balloon house. The police of the prince had with difficulty cleared the boulevard between the seawall and the wide-open doors. Assistants and supernumeraries leaned over the wall with outstretched arms waiting for me; below on the beach were others; but this time I did not need them. I slowed the speed of the propeller as I came to them. Just as I was halfway over the seawall, well above them all, I stopped the motor. Carried onward by the dying momentum, the airship glided over their heads on toward the open door. They had grasped my guide rope, to draw me down, but as I had been coming diagonally, there was no need of it. Now they walked beside the airship into the balloon house, as its trainer or the stable boys grasp the bridle of their racehorse after the course and lead him back in honor to the stable with his jockey in the saddle!

It was admitted, nevertheless, that I ought not to be obliged to steer so closely on returning from my flights — to enter the aerodrome as a needle is threaded by a steady hand — because a side gust of wind might catch me at the critical moment and dash me against a tree or lamp post or telegraph or telephone pole, not to speak of the sharp-cornered buildings on either side of the aerodrome. When I went out again for a short spin that same afternoon of January 29, 1902, the obstruction of the seawall made itself only too evident. The prince offered to tear down the wall.

"I will not ask you to do so much," I said. "It will be enough to build a landing stage on the sea side of the wall, at the level of the boulevard."

This was done after twelve days of work interrupted by persistent rain, and the airship, when it issued for its third flight, on February 10, 1902, had simply to be lifted a few feet by men on each side of the wall. They drew it gently on until its whole length floated in equilibrium over the new platform that extended so far out into the surf that its farthermost piles were always in six feet of water.

Standing on this platform, they steadied the airship while its motor was being started, while I let out the overplus of water ballast and shifted my guide rope so as to point for an oblique drive upward. The motor began spitting and rumbling. The propeller began turning.

"Let go, all!" I cried for the third time at Monaco.

Lightly the airship slid along its oblique course onward and upward. Then, as the propeller gathered force, a mighty push sent me flying over the bay. I shifted front the guide rope again to make a level course. And out to sea the airship darted, its scarlet pennant fluttering symbolic letters as upon a streak of flame. They were the initial letters of the first line of Camoën's *Lusiad,* the epic poet of my race:

"Por mares nunca d'antes navegados!"
("O'er seas heretofore unsailed!")

33. Santos-Dumont being lifted over the sea wall

34. The "Santos-Dumont No. 7"

CHAPTER XVIII

FLIGHTS IN
MEDITERRANEAN WINDS

In my two previous experiments I had kept fairly within the wind protected limits of the Bay of Monaco, whose broad expanse afforded ample room both for guide-roping and practice in steering. Furthermore, a hundred friends and thousands of friendly spectators stood around it from the terraces of Monte Carlo to the shore of La Condamine and up the other side to the heights of Old Monaco. As I circled round and round the bay, mounted obliquely and swooped down, fetched a straight course and then stopped abruptly to turn and begin again, their applause came up to me agreeably. Now, on my third flight, I steered for the open sea.

Out into the open Mediterranean I sped. The guide rope held me at a steady altitude of about fifty meters above the waves, as if in some mysterious way its lower end were attached to them.

In this way, automatically secure of my altitude, I found the work of aerial navigation become wonderfully easy. There was no ballast to throw out, no gas to let out, no shifting of the weights except when I expressly desired to mount or descend. So, with my hand upon the rudder and my eye fixed on the far-off point of Cap Martin, I gave myself up to the pleasure of this voyaging above the waves.

Here in these azure solitudes there were no chimney pots of Paris, no cruel, threatening roof corners, no treetops of the Bois de Boulogne. My propeller was showing its power and I was free to let it go. I had only to hold my course straight in the teeth of the breeze and watch the far-off Mediterranean shore flit past me.

I had plenty of leisure to look about. Presently I met two sailing yachts scudding toward me down the coast. I noticed that their sails were full-bellied. As I flew on, I heard a faint cheer, and a graceful female figure on the foremost yacht waved a red foulard. As I turned to answer the politeness, I perceived with some astonishment that we were far apart already.

I was now well up the coast, about halfway to Cap Martin. Above was the limitless blue void. Below was the solitude of white-capped waves. From the appearance of sailing boats here and there, I could tell that the wind was increasing to a squall and I should have to turn in it, before I could fly back upon it in my homeward trip.

Porting my helm, I held the rudder tight. The airship swung round like a boat; then, as the wind sent me flying down the coast, my only work was to maintain the steady course. In scarcely more time than it takes to write it, I was opposite the Bay of Monaco again.

With a sharp turn of the rudder I entered the protected harbor and, amid a thousand cheers, stopped the propeller, pulled in the forward shifting weight, and let the dying impetus of the airship carry it diagonally down to the landing stage. This time there was no trouble. On the broad landing stage stood my own men, assisted by those put at my disposition by the prince. The airship was grasped as it came gliding slowly to them; and, without actually coming to a stop, it was "led" over the seawall across the Boulevard de la Condamine and into the aerodrome. The trip had lasted less than an hour and I had been within a few hundred yards of Cap Martin.

Here was an obvious trip, first against and then with a stiff wind; and the curious may render themselves an account of the fact by glancing at the photographs marked "Wind A," and "Wind B." As they happened to be taken by a Monte Carlo professional intent simply on getting good photographs, they are impartial.

"Wind A" shows me leaving the Bay of Monaco against a wind that is blowing back the smoke of the two steamers seen on the horizon.

"Wind B" was taken up the coast, just before I met the two little sailing yachts which are obviously scudding toward me.

The loneliness in which I found myself in the middle of this first extended flight up the Mediterranean shore was not part of the program. During the manufacture of the hydrogen gas and the filling of the balloon, I had received the visits of a great many promi-

35.   "Wind A" and "Wind B"

36. From the balloon house at La Condamine, February 12, 1902

nent people, several of whom signified their ability and readiness to lend valuable aid to these experiments. From Beaulieu, where his steam yacht *Lysistrata* was at anchor, came Mr. James Gordon Bennett, and Mr. Eugene Higgins had already brought the *Varuna* up from Nice on more than one occasion. The beautiful little steam yacht of M. Eiffel also held itself in readiness.

It had been the intention of these owners, as it had been that of the prince with his *Princesse Alice,* to follow the airship in its flights over the Mediterranean so as to be on the spot in case of accident. This first flight, however, had been taken on impulse before any program for the yachts had been arranged, and my next long flight, as will be seen, demonstrated that this kind of protection must not be counted on overmuch by airship captains.

It was on February 12, 1902. One steam chaloupe and two petroleum launches, all three of them swift goers, together with three well-manned rowboats, had been stationed at intervals down the coast to pick me up in case of accident. The steam chaloupe of the Prince of Monaco, carrying his Highness, the Governor-General, and the captain of the *Princesse Alice,* had already started on the course ahead of time. The 40 horsepower Mors automobile of Mr. Clarence Grey Dinsmore and the 30 horsepower Panhard of M. Isidore Kahenstein were prepared to follow along the lower coast road.

Immediately on leaving the Bay of Monaco I met the wind head on, as I steered my course straight down the coast in the direction of the Italian frontier. Putting on all speed, I held the rudder firm and let myself go. I could see the ragged outlines of the coast flit past me on the left. Along the winding road the two racing automobiles kept abreast with me, being driven at high speed.

"It was all we could do to follow the airship along the curves of the coast road," said one of Mr. Dinsmore's passengers to the reporter of a Paris journal, "so rapid was its flight. In less than five minutes it had arrived opposite the Villa Camille Blanc, which is about three quarters of a mile distant from Cap Martin as the crow flies.

"At this moment the airship was absolutely alone. Between it and Cap Martin I saw a single rowboat, while far behind was visible the smoke from the prince's chaloupe. It was really no commonplace sight to see the airship thus hovering, isolated, over the immense sea."

The wind, instead of subsiding had been increasing. Here and there around the horizon I could see the bent white sails of yachts driven before it. The situation was new to me, so I made an abrupt turn and started back on the home stretch.

Now again the wind was with me, stronger than it had been on the preceding flight down the coast. Yet it was easy steering, and I remarked with pleasure that going thus with the wind the pitching, or *tangage,* of the airship was much less. Though going fast with my propeller, and aided by the wind behind me, I felt no more motion — indeed, even less — than before.

For the rest, how different were my sensations from those of the spherical balloonist! It is true that he sees the earth flying backward beneath him at tremendous speed. But he knows that he is powerless. The great sphere of gas above him is the plaything of the air current; and he cannot change his direction by a hairsbreadth. In my airship I could see myself flying over the sea, but I had my hands on a helm that made me master of my direction in this splendid course. Once or twice, merely to give myself an account of it, I shoved the helm around a short arc. Obedient, the airship's stem swung to the other side, and I found myself speeding in a new diagonal course. But these maneuvers occupied only a few instants each, and each time I swung myself back on a straight line to the entrance to the Bay of Monaco, for I was flying homeward like an eagle, and must keep my course.

To those watching my return from the terraces of Monte Carlo and Monaco town, as they told me afterward, the airship increased in size at every instant, like a veritable eagle bearing down upon them. As the wind was coming toward them, they could hear the low crackling rumble of my motor a long distance off. Faintly, now, their own shouts of encouragement came to me. Almost instantly the shouts grew loud. Around the bay a thousand handkerchiefs were fluttering. I gave a sharp turn to the helm, and the airship leaped into the bay, amid the cheering and the waving, just as rain began to fall.[1]

I had first slowed and then stopped the motor. As the airship now slowly approached the landing stage, borne on by its dying momentum, I gave the usual signal for those in the boats to seize my guide rope. The steam chaloupe of the prince, which had turned

[1]"Half an hour after the aeronaut's return the wind became violent, a heavy storm followed, and the sea became very rough." (Paris edition, *New York Herald,* February 13, 1902.)

back midway between Monte Carlo and Cap Martin after I had overtaken and passed it on my out trip, had by this time reached the bay. The prince, who was still on board, desired to catch the guide rope; and those with him, having no experience of its weight and the force with which the airship drags it through the water, did not seek to dissuade him. Instead of catching the heavy, floating cordage as the darting chaloupe passed it, His Highness managed to get struck by it on the right arm, an accident which knocked him fairly to the bottom of the little vessel and produced severe contusions.

A second attempt to catch the guide rope was more successful, and the airship was easily drawn to the seawall, over it, and into its house. Like everything in this new navigation, the particular maneuver was new. I was still going faster than I appeared to be, and such attempts to catch and stop an airship even on its dying momentum are apt to upset someone. The only way not to get too abrupt a shock is to run with the machine and slow it down gently.

CHAPTER XIX

SPEED

What speed my "No. 6" made on these Mediterranean flights was not published at the time because I had not sought to calculate it closely. Fresh from the troubling time limit of the Deutsch Prize competition, I amused myself frankly with my airship, making observations of great value to myself, but not seeking to prove anything to anyone.

The speed problem is, doubtless, the first of all airship problems, and until high speed shall be arrived at, certain other problems of aerial navigation must remain in part unsolved. For example, take that of the airship's pitching *(tangage)*. I think it quite likely that a critical point in speed will be found, beyond which, on each side, the pitching will be practically nil. When going slowly or at moderate speed I have experienced no pitching, which in an airship like my "No. 6" seems always to commence at 25 to 30 kilometers (15 to 18 miles) per hour through the air. Now, probably, when one passes this speed considerably — say at the rate of 50 kilometers (30 miles) per hour — all *tangage,* or pitching, will be found to cease again, as I myself found when flying homeward on the wind in the voyage described in the last chapter.

Speed must always be the final test between rival airships, because in itself speed sums up all other airship qualities, including "stability." At Monaco, however, I had no rivals to compete with. Furthermore, my prime study and amusement there was the beautiful working of the maritime guide rope, and this guide rope, dragging through the water, must of necessity retard whatever speed I made. There could be no help for it. Such was the price I must pay for automatic equilibrium and vertical stability — in a word, easy navigation — so long as I remained the sole and solitary navigator of the airship.

Nor is it an easy task to calculate an airship's speed. On these flights up and down the Mediterranean coast, the speed of my return to Monaco, wonderfully aided by the wind, could bear no relation to the speed out, retarded by the wind, and there was nothing to show that the force of the wind, going and coming, was constant. It is true that on those flights one of the difficulties standing in the way of such speed calculations — the "shoot the chutes" *(montagnes Russes)* of ever-varying altitude — was done away with by the operation of the maritime guide rope; but, on the other hand, as has been said, the dragging of the guide rope's weight through the water acted as a very effectual brake. As the speed of the airship is increased, this brake-like action of the guide rope (like that of the resistance of the atmosphere itself) grows, not in proportion to the speed, but in proportion to the square of it.

On these flights along the Mediterranean coast the easy navigation afforded me by the maritime guide rope was purchased, as nearly as I could calculate, by the sacrifice of about 7 or 8 kilometers (4 or 5 miles) per hour of speed; but with or without maritime guide rope, the speed calculation has its own almost insurmountable difficulties.

From Monte Carlo to Cap Martin at 10 o'clock of a given morning may be quite a different trip from Monte Carlo to Cap Martin at noon of the same day; while from Cap Martin to Monte Carlo, except in perfect calm, must always be a still different proposition. Nor can any accurate calculations be based on the markings of the anemometer, an instrument which I nevertheless carried. Out of simple curiosity I made note of its readings on several occasions during my trip of February 12, 1902. It seemed to be marking between 32 and 37 kilometers (20 and 23 miles) per hour; but the wind, complicated by side gusts, acting at the same time on the airship and the wings of the anemometer windmill — *i.e.,* on two moving systems whose inertia cannot possibly be compared — would alone be sufficient to falsify the result.

When, therefore, I state that, according to my best judgment, the average of my speed through the air on these flights was between 30 and 35 kilometers (18 and 22 miles) per hour, it will be understood that it refers to speed through the air whether the air be still or moving, and to speed retarded by the dragging of the maritime guide rope. Putting this adverse influence at the moderate figure of 7 kilometers (4½ miles) per hour, my speed through the still or moving air would be between 37 and 42 kilometers (22 and 27 miles) per hour.

Rather than spend time over illusory calculations on paper, I have always preferred to go on materially improving my airships. Later, when they come in competition with the rivals which no one awaits more ardently than myself, all speed calculations made on paper and all disputes based on them must of necessity yield to the one sublime test of airship racing!

Where speed calculations have their real importance is in affording necessary data for the construction of new and more powerful airships. Thus the balloon of my racing "No. 7," whose motive power depends on two propellers each 5 meters (16½ feet) in diameter and worked by a 60 horsepower motor, with a water cooler, has its envelop made of two layers of the strongest French silk, four times varnished, capable of standing, under dynamometric test, a traction of 3000 kilograms (6600 pounds) for the linear meter. I will now try to explain why the balloon envelop must be made so very much stronger as the speed of the airship is designed to be increased; and in so doing, I shall have to reveal the unique and paradoxical danger that besets high-speed dirigibles, threatening them, not with beating their heads in against the outer atmosphere, but with blowing their tails out behind them!

Although the interior pressure in the balloons of my airships is very considerable, as balloons go — the spherical balloon, having a hole in its bottom, is under no such pressure — it is so little in comparison with the general pressure of the atmosphere that we measure it, not by "atmospheres," but by centimeters or millimeters of water pressure — *i.e.,* the pressure that will send a column of water up that distance in a tube. One "atmosphere" means 1 kilogram of pressure to the square centimeter, or 15 pounds to the square inch, and it is equivalent to about 10 meters of water pressure, or more conveniently, 1000 centimeters of water. Now, supposing the interior pressure in my slower "No. 6" to have been close up to 3 centimeters of water (it required that pressure to open its gas valves), it would have been equivalent to 1/333 of an atmosphere; and as 1 atmosphere is equivalent to a pressure of 1000 grams (1 kilogram) on 1 square centimeter, the interior pressure of my "No. 6" would have been 1/333 of 1000 grams, or 3 grams.

Therefore on 1 square meter (10,000 square centimeters) of the stem head of the balloon of my "No. 6," the interior pressure would have been 10,000 multiplied by 3, or 30,000 grams — *i.e.,* 30 kilograms, or 66 pounds.

How is this interior pressure maintained without being exceeded? Were the great exterior balloon filled with hydrogen and then sealed up with wax at each of its valves, the sun's heat might expand the hydrogen, making it exceed this pressure and bursting the balloon; or should the sealed balloon rise high, the decreasing pressure of the outer atmosphere might let its hydrogen expand, with the same result. The gas valves of the great balloon, therefore, must *not* be sealed; and, furthermore, they must always be very carefully made, so that they will open of their own accord at the required and calculated pressure.

This pressure (of 3 centimeters in the "No. 6"), it ought to be noted, is attained by the heating of the sun or by a rise in altitude only when the balloon is completely filled with gas; what may be called its working pressure — about one-fifth lower — is maintained by the rotary air pump. Worked continually by the motor, it pumps air constantly into the small interior balloon. As much of this air as is needed to preserve the outer balloon's rigidity remains inside the little interior balloon, but all the rest pushes its way out into the atmosphere again through its air valve, which opens at a little less pressure than do the gas valves.

Let us now return to the balloon of my "No. 6." The *interior* pressure on each square meter of its stem head being continuously about 30 kilograms, the silk material composing it must be normally strong enough to stand it; nevertheless, it will be easy to see how it becomes more and more relieved of that interior pressure as the airship gets in motion and increases speed. Its striking against the atmosphere makes a counter pressure *against the outside* of the stem head. Up to 30 kilograms to the square meter, therefore, all increase in the airship's speed tends to reduce strain, so that the faster the airship goes, the less will it be liable to burst its head!

How fast may the balloon be carried on by motor and propeller before its head stem strikes the atmosphere hard enough to more than neutralize the interior pressure? This, too, is a matter of calculation; but to spare the reader, I will content myself with pointing out that my flights over the Mediterranean proved that the balloon of my "No. 6" could safely stand a speed of 42 kilometers (22 to 27 miles) per hour without giving the slightest hint of strain. Had I wanted an airship of the proportions of the "No. 6" to go twice as fast, under the same conditions, its balloon must have been strong enough to stand four times its interior pressure of 3 centimeters of "water," because the resistance of the atmosphere grows, not in proportion to the speed, but in proportion to the square of the speed.

The balloon of my "No. 7" is not, of course, built in the precise proportions as that of my "No. 6"; but I may mention that it has been tested to resist an interior pressure of much more than 12 centimeters of "water" — in fact, its gas valves open at that pressure only. This means just four times the interior pressure of my "No. 6." Comparing the two balloons in a general way, it is obvious, therefore, that with no risk from outside pressure and, with positive relief from interior pressure on its stem or head, the balloon of my "No. 7" may be driven twice as fast as my easygoing Mediterranean pace of 42 kilometers (25 miles) per hour — or fifty miles!

This brings us to the unique and paradoxical weakness of the fast-going dirigible. Up to the point where the exterior shall equal the interior pressure, we have seen how every increase of speed actually guarantees safety to the stem of the balloon. Unhappily, it does not remain true of the balloon's stern head. On it the interior pressure is also continuous, but speed cannot relieve it. On the contrary, the *suction* of the atmosphere behind the balloon as it speeds on increases also, almost in the same proportion as the pressure caused by driving the balloon against the atmosphere. And this suction, instead of operating to neutralize the interior pressure on the balloon's stern head, *increases* the strain just that much, the pull being added to the push. Paradoxical as it may seem, therefore, the danger of the swift dirigible is to blow its tail out rather than its head in! (Figure 12.)

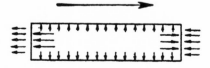

Figure Twelve

How is this danger to be met? Obviously, by strengthening the stern part of the balloon envelop. We have seen that when the

speed of my "No. 7" shall be just great enough to completely neutralize the interior pressure on its stem or head, the strain on its
stern head will be doubled. For this reason I have doubled the balloon material at this point.

I have reason to be careful of the balloon of my "No. 7." In it
the speed problem will be attacked definitively. It has two propellers, each 5 meters (16½ feet) in diameter. One will push, as usual,
from the stern, while the other will pull from the stem, as in my
"No. 4." Its 60 horsepower Clément motor will — if my expec-
tations are fulfilled — give it a speed of between 70 and 80 kilometers
(40 and 50 miles) per hour. In a word, the speed of my "No. 7" will
bring us very close to practical everyday aerial navigation, for as we
seldom have a wind blowing as much, even, as 50 kilometers (30
miles) per hour, such an airship will surely be able to go out daily
during more than ten months in the twelve.

CHAPTER XX

AN ACCIDENT AND ITS LESSONS

At half-past two o'clock in the afternoon of February 14, 1902, the stanch airship which won the Deutsch Prize left the aerodrome of La Condamine on what was destined to be its last voyage.

Immediately on quitting the aerodrome it began behaving badly, dipping heavily. It had left the balloon house imperfectly inflated; hence it lacked ascensional force. To keep my proper altitude, I increased its diagonal pointing and kept the propeller pushing it on upward. The dipping, of course, was due to the counter effort of gravity.

In the shaded atmosphere of the aerodrome the air had been comparatively cool. The balloon was now out in the hot open sunlight. As a consequence, the hydrogen nearest to the silk cover rarefied rapidly. As the balloon had left the aerodrome imperfectly inflated, the rarefied hydrogen was able to rush to the highest possible point, the up-pointing stem. This exaggerated the inclination which I had made purposely. The balloon pointed higher and higher. Indeed, for a time it seemed almost to be pointing perpendicularly.

Before I had time to correct this "rearing up" of my aerial steed, many of the diagonal wires had begun to give way, as the slanting pressure on them was unusual, and others, including those of the rudder, caught in the propeller.

Should I leave the propeller to grind on the rigging, the balloon envelop would be torn the next moment, the gas would leave the balloon in a mass, and I would be precipitated into the waves with violence.

I stopped the motor. I was now in the position of an ordinary spherical balloonist, at the mercy of the winds. These were taking

Phase A

Phase B

37.   Accident, February 14, 1902.

Phase C

Phase D, before final collapse

38. Accident, February 14, 1902.

me inshore, where I would be presently cast upon the telegraph wires, trees, and house corners of Monte Carlo.

There was but one thing to do.

Pulling on the maneuver valve, I let out a sufficient quantity of hydrogen and came slowly down to the surface of the water, in which the airship sank.

Balloon, keel, and motor were successfully fished up the next day and shipped off to Paris for repairs. Thus abruptly ended my maritime experiments; but thus also I learned that, while a properly inflated balloon, furnished with the proper valves, has nothing to fear from gas displacement, it is best to be on the safe side and guard oneself against the possibility of such displacement when by some neglect or other the balloon is allowed to go out imperfectly inflated.

For this reason, in all my succeeding airships the balloon is divided into many compartments by vertical silk partitions, not varnished. The partitions remaining unvarnished, the hydrogen gas can slowly pass through their meshes from one compartment to another, to insure an equal pressure throughout. But as they are, nevertheless, partitions, they are always ready to guard against any precipitous rushing of gas toward either extremity of the balloon.

Indeed, the experimenter with dirigible balloons must be continually on his guard against little errors and neglects of his aids. I have four men who have now been with me four years. They are in their way experts, and I have every confidence in them. Yet this thing happened: the airship was allowed to leave the aerodrome imperfectly inflated. Imagine, then, what might be the danger of an experimenter with a set of inexperienced subordinates!

In spite of their great simplicity, my airships require constant surveillance on a few capital heads.

Is the balloon properly filled?

Is there any possibility of a leak?

Is the rigging in condition?

Is the motor in condition?

Do the cords commanding rudder, motor, water ballast, and the shifting guide rope work freely?

Is the ballast properly weighed?

Looked on as a mere machine, the airship requires no more care than an automobile, but from the point of view of consequences, the need of faithful and intelligent surveillance is simply imperious. This very day the highways of all France are dotted with a thousand automobiles *en panne,* with their enthusiastic drivers crawling underneath them in the dust, oil-can and wrench in hand, repairing momentary accidents. They think no less of their automobile for this reason. Yet let the airship have the same trifling accident, and all the world is likely to hear of the fact!

In the first years of my experiments, I insisted on doing everything for myself. I "groomed" my balloons and motors with my own hands. My present aids understand my present airships, and nine times out of ten they hand them over to me in good condition for the voyage. Yet were I to begin experiments with a new type, I should have to train them all anew, and during that time I should have to care for the airships with my own hands again.

On this occasion, the airship left the aerodrome imperfectly weighed and inflated, not so much by the neglect of my men as by reason of the imperfect situation of the aerodrome. In spite of the care that had been given to designing and constructing it, from the very nature of its situation there was no space outside in which to send up the airship and ascertain if its ballast were properly distributed. Could this have been done, the imperfect inflation of the balloon would have been perceived in time.

Looking back over all my varied experiences, I reflect with astonishment that one of my greatest dangers passed unperceived even by myself at the end of my most successful flight over the Mediterranean.

It was at the time the prince attempted to grasp my guide rope and was knocked into the bottom of his steam chaloupe. I had entered the bay after flying homeward up the coast, and they were towing me toward the aerodrome. The airship had descended very close to the surface of the water, and they were pulling it still lower by means of the guide rope, until it was not many feet above the smokestack of the steam chaloupe — and that smokestack was belching red-hot sparks!

Any one of those red-hot sparks might have, ascending, burnt a hole in my balloon, set fire to the hydrogen, and blown balloon and myself to atoms!

CHAPTER XXI

THE FIRST OF THE WORLD'S AIRSHIP STATIONS

Airship experimenters labor under one peculiar disadvantage quite apart from the proper difficulties of the problem. It is due to the utter newness of travel in a third dimension, and consists in the slowness with which our minds realize the necessity of providing for the diagonal mountings and descents of the airships, starting from and returning to the ground.

When the Aéro Club of Paris laid out its grounds at Saint Cloud, it was with the sole idea of facilitating the vertical mounting of spherical balloons. Indeed, no provisions were made, even, for the landing of spherical balloons, because their captains never hoped to bring them back to the Saint Cloud Balloon Park otherwise than by rail, packed in their boxes. The spherical balloon lands where the wind takes it.

When I built my first airship house in the club's grounds at Saint Cloud, I dare say that the then novel advantages of possessing my own gas plant, workshop, and a shelter in which the inflated dirigibles could be housed indefinitely withheld my attention from this other almost vital problem of surroundings. It was already a great progress for me not to be obliged to empty the balloon and waste its hydrogen at the end of each trip. Thus I was content to build, simply, an airship house with great sliding doors, without even taking precautions to guarantee a flat, open space in front and, less still, on either side of it. When, little by little, trenches something like a yard deep — vague foundation outlines for constructions that were never finished — began appearing here and there, to the right of my open doors and on beyond, I realized that my aids might risk falling into them in running to catch my guide rope when I should be returning from a trip. And when the gigantic skeleton of M. Henri Deutsch's airship house, designed to shelter the airship he built on the lines of my "No. 6," and called "La Ville de Paris," rose directly in front of my sliding doors and scarcely two airship's lengths distant from them, it dawned on me at last that here was something of a peril and more than a simple inconvenience due to natural crowding in a club's grounds. In spite of the new peril, the Deutsch Prize was won. Returning from the Eiffel Tower I passed high above the skeleton. I may say here, however, that the foundation trenches innocently caused the painful controversy about my time to which I have made a brief allusion in the chapter. Seeing that they might easily break their legs by stumbling into those foundation trenches, I had positively forbidden my men to run across that space to catch my guide rope with their eyes and arms up in the air. Not dreaming that such a point could be raised, my men obeyed the injunction. Observing that I was quite master of my rudder, motor, and propeller, able to turn and return to the spot where the judges stood, they let me pass on over their heads without seeking to catch and run along with the guide rope, a thing they might have done easily — at the risk of their legs!

Again at Monaco, after a well-planned airship house had been erected in what seemed an ideal spot, we have seen what dangers were, nevertheless, threatened by the seawall, the Boulevard de la Condamine with its poles, wires, and traffic, and the final disaster due entirely to the absence of a weighing ground beside the aerodrome. These are dangers and inconveniences against which we come in time to be on our guard by actual and often dire experience.

During the spring and summer of 1902 I took trips to England and the United States, of which I shall have a word to say later. Returning from these trips to Paris, I at once set about selecting the site of an aerodrome that should be all my own and in which the experience gained at such cost should be taken advantage of. This time, I resolved, my airship house should have an ample space around it. And, succeeding in a way, I realized — if I may say it — the first of the airship stations of the future.

After long search, I came on a fair-sized lot of vacant ground surrounded by a high stone wall, inside the police jurisdiction of the Bois de Boulogne but private property, situated on the Rue de Longchamps, in Neuilly Saint James. First, I had to come to an under-

39. Airship station, Neuilly St. James

40. "The Omnibus"

standing with its owner. Then I had to come to an understanding with the Bois authorities, who took time to give a building permit to such an unusual construction as a house from which airships would go and come.

The Rue de Longchamps is a narrow suburban street, little built on at this end, that gives on the Bagatelle gate to the Bois de Boulogne beside the training ground of the same name. To go and come in my airships from this side is, however, inconvenient because of the walls of the various properties, the trees that line the Bois so thickly, and the great park gates. To the right and left of my little property are other buildings. Behind me, across the Boulevard de la Seine, is the river itself, with the Île de Puteaux in it. It is from this side that I must go and come in my airships. Mounting diagonally in the air from my own open grounds, I pass over my wall, the Boulevard de la Seine, and turn when well above the river. Regularly I turn to the left and make my way, in a great arc, to the Bois by way of the training ground, itself a fairly open space.

There it stands in its grounds, the first of the airship stations of the future, capable of housing seven airships all inflated and prepared to navigate at an instant's notice! But, in spite of all the needs that I attempted to provide for in it, what a small and hampered place it is, compared with the great highly organized stations which the future must produce for itself, with their high-placed and spacious landing stages to which airships will descend with complete safety and convenience, like great birds that seek nests on flat rocks! Such stations may have little car tracks running out from their interior to the wide landing spaces. The cars that run over them will pull the airships in and out by their guide ropes, without loss of time or the aid of a dozen or more men. Their observation towers will serve for judges' timing stations in aerial races; fitted with wireless telegraph apparatus, they may be able to communicate with distant goals and, perhaps, even with the airships in motion. Attached to their airship stations there will be gas generating plants. There may be a casemated workshop for the testing of motors. There will certainly be sleeping rooms for experimenters who desire to make an early start and profit by the calm of the dawn. It is quite probable that there will also be balloon envelop workshops for repairs and changes — a carpenter shop and a machine shop with intelligent and experienced workmen ready and able to seize an idea and execute it.

Meanwhile, my airship station of the present is said to resemble a great square tent, striped red and white, set in the midst of a vacant lot surrounded by a high stone wall. Its tent-like appearance is due to the fact that, being in a hurry to utilize it, I saw no reason to construct its walls or roof of wood. The framework consists of long rows of parallel wooden pillars. Across their tops is stretched a canvas roof, and the four sides are made of the same striped canvas. This makes a construction stronger than at first appears, the outside tent-stuff weighing some 2600 kilograms (5720 pounds), and being sustained between the pillars by metallic cordage.

Inside, the central stalls are 31 feet wide, 165 feet long, and 44½ feet high, affording room for the largest dirigibles without permitting them to come into contact with each other. The great sliding doors are but a repetition of those of Monaco.

When, in the spring of 1903, I found my airship station completed, I had three new airships ready to house in it. They were:

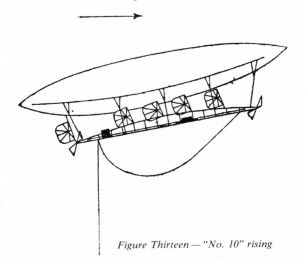

Figure Thirteen — "No. 10" rising

My "No. 7." This I call my racing airship. It is designed and reserved for important competitions, the mere cost of filling it with hydrogen being more than three thousand francs. It is true that, once filled, it may be kept inflated for a month at the expense of fifty francs per day for hydrogen to replace what is lost. Having a gas capacity of 1257 cubic meters (nearly 45,000 cubic feet) it possesses twice the lifting power of my "No. 6," in which the Deutsch Prize was won; and such is the necessary weight of its 60 horsepower water-cooled four-cylinder motor and its proportionally strong machinery that I shall probably take up no more ballast in it than I took up in the "No. 6." Comparing their sizes and lifting powers, it would make five of my "No. 9," the novel little "run-about," which I shall describe in the succeeding chapter.

The third of the new airships is:

My "No. 10," which has been called "The Omnibus." Its gas capacity of 2010 cubic meters (nearly 80,000 cubic feet) makes its balloon greater in size and lifting power than even the racing "No.

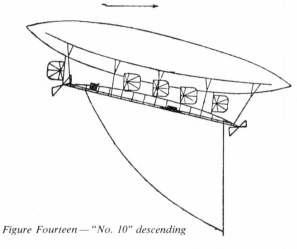

Figure Fourteen — "No. 10" descending

7"; and should I, indeed, desire at any time to shift to it the latter's keel, all furnished with the racing motor and machinery, I might combine a very swift aircraft capable of carrying myself, several aids, a large supply of both petroleum and ballast — not to speak of war munitions, were the sudden need of a belligerent character.

The prime purpose of my "No. 10," however, is well indicated in its name "The Omnibus." Its keel, or rather keels, as I have fashioned them, are double. That is to say, hanging underneath its usual keel, in which my basket is situated, there is a passenger keel that holds three similar baskets and a smaller one for my aid. Each passenger basket is large enough to hold four passengers; and it is to carry such passengers that "The Omnibus" has been constructed.

Indeed, after mature reflection, it seemed to me that this must be the most practical and rapid way to popularize aerial navigation.

In my other airships I have shown that it is possible to mount and travel through the air on a prescribed course with no greater danger than one risks in any racing automobile. In "The Omnibus" I shall demonstrate to the world that there are very many men and women possessed of sufficient confidence in the aerial idea to mount with me as passengers in the first of the air omnibuses of the future!

CHAPTER XXII

MY "NO. 9," THE LITTLE RUNABOUT

Once I was enamoured of high power petroleum automobiles: they can go at express train speed to any part of Europe, finding fuel in any village. "I can go to Moscow or Lisbon!" I said to myself. But when I discovered that I did not want to go to Moscow or to Lisbon, the small and handy electric runabout in which I do my errands about Paris and the Bois proved more satisfactory.

Speaking from the standpoint of my pleasure and convenience as a Parisian, my airship experience has been similar. When the balloon and motor of my 60 horsepower "No. 7" were completed, I said to myself:

"I can race any airship that is likely to be built!" But when I found that, in spite of the forfeits I paid into the Aéro Club's treasury, there was no one ready to race with me, I determined to build a small airship runabout for my pleasure and convenience only. In it I would pass the time while waiting for the future to bring forth competitions worthy of my racecraft.

So I built my "No. 9," the smallest of possible dirigibles, yet very practical indeed. As originally constructed, its balloon's capacity was but 220 cubic meters (7770 cubic feet), permitting me to take up less than 30 kilograms (66 pounds) of ballast; and thus I navigated it for weeks, without inconvenience. Even when I enlarged its balloon to 261 cubic meters (9218 cubic feet) the balloon of my "No. 6," in which I won the Deutsch Prize, would have made almost three of it, while that of my "Omnibus" is fully eight times its size. As I have already stated, its 3 horsepower Clément motor weighs but 12 kilograms (26½ pounds). With such a motor one cannot expect great speed; nevertheless, this handy little runabout takes me over the Bois at between 20 and 25 kilometers (12 and 15 miles) per hour, and this notwithstanding its egg-shaped form (Figure 15), which would seemingly be little calculated for cutting the air. Indeed, to make it respond promptly to the rudder, I drive it thick end first.

I have said that, as it was originally proportioned, 'the balloon of this smallest of possible dirigibles permitted me to take up less than 30 kilograms (66 pounds) of ballast. As now enlarged, its lifting power is greater; but when account is taken of my own weight and the weight of keel, motor, screw, and machinery, the whole system becomes neither lighter nor heavier than the surrounding atmos-

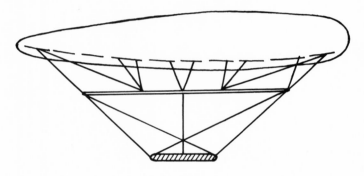

Figure Fifteen

phere when I have loaded it with 60 kilograms (132 pounds) of ballast. And it is just in this connection that it will be easiest to explain why I have called this little airship very practical. On Monday, June 29, 1903, I landed with it on the grounds of the Aéro Club at Saint Cloud, in the midst of six inflated spherical balloons. After a short call, I started off again.

"Can we not give you some gas?" politely asked my fellow clubmen.

"You saw me coming all the way from Neuilly," I replied. "Did I throw out any ballast?"

"You threw out no ballast," they admitted.

"Then why should I be in need of gas?"

As a matter of scientific curiosity, I may relate that I did not either lose or sacrifice a cubic foot of gas or a single pound of ballast that whole afternoon; nor has that experience been at all ex-

41.   The "Santos-Dumont No. 9" over the Bois de Boulogne

42.   Santos-Dumont lands at his own front door

ceptional in the very practical little "No. 9," or even in its predecessors. It will be remembered that on the day succeeding the winning of the Deutsch Prize my chief mechanic found that the balloon of my "No. 6" would take no gas, because none had been lost.

After leaving my fellow clubmen at Saint Cloud that afternoon, I made a typically practical trip. To go from Neuilly Saint James to the Aéro Club's grounds I had already passed the Seine. Now, crossing it again, I made the café-restaurant of "The Cascade," where I stopped for refreshments. It was by this time 5 P.M. Not wishing to return yet to my station, I crossed the Seine for a third time and went in a straight course as close to the great fort of Mont Valérien as delicacy permitted. Then, returning, I traversed the river once again and came to earth in my own grounds at Neuilly.

During the whole trip my greatest altitude was 105 meters (346 feet). Taking into consideration that my guide rope hangs 132 feet below me and that the tops of the Bois trees extend up some 70 feet from the ground, this extreme altitude left me but 140 feet of clear space for vertical maneuvering.

It was enough, and the proof of it is that I do not go higher on these trips of pleasure and experiment. Indeed, when I hear of dirigibles going up 1300 feet in the air without some special justifying object, I am filled with amazement. As I have already explained, the place of the dirigible is, normally, in low altitudes; and the ideal is to guide rope on a sufficiently low course to be left free from vertical maneuvering. This is what M. Armengaud *jeune* referred to in his learned inaugural discourse delivered before the Société Française de Navigation Aérienne in 1901, when he advised me to quit the Mediterranean and go guide roping over great plains like that of La Beauce.

It is not necessary to go to the Plain of La Beauce. One can guide rope even in the center of Paris if one goes about it at the proper moment. I have done it.

I have guide roped round the Arc de Triomphe and down the Avenue des Champs Élysées at a lower altitude than the housetops on either side, fearing no ill and finding no difficulty. My first flight of this kind occurred when I sought for the first time to land in my "No. 9" in front of my own house door at the corner of the Avenue des Champs Élysées and the Rue Washington, on Tuesday, June 23, 1903.

Knowing that the feat must be accomplished at an hour when

the imposing pleasure promenade of Paris would be least encumbered, I had instructed my men to sleep through the early part of the night in the airship station at Neuilly Saint James, so as to be able to have the "No. 9" ready for an early start at dawn. I myself rose at 2 A.M., and in my handy electric automobile arrived at the station while it was yet dark. The men still slept. I climbed the wall, waked them, and succeeded in quitting the earth on my first diagonally upward course over the wall and above the river Seine before the day had broken. Turning to the left, I made my way across the Bois, picking out the open spaces so as to guide rope as much as possible.

When I came to trees, I jumped over them. So, navigating through the cool air of the delicious dawn, I reached the Porte Dauphine and the beginning of the broad Avenue du Bois de Boulogne, which leads directly to the Arc de Triomphe. This carriage promenade of Tout-Paris was absolutely empty.

"I will guide rope up the Avenue of the Bois!" I said to myself gleefully.

What this means you will perceive when I recall that my guide rope's length is barely 132 feet, and that one guide ropes best with 66 feet of it trailing along the ground. Thus I went lower than the roofs of many houses on each side. I call this practical airship navigation because:

(*a*) It leaves the aerial navigator free to steer his course without pitching and without care or effort to maintain his steady altitude.

(*b*) It can be done with absolute safety from falling, not only to the navigator, but also to the airship — a consideration not without its merit when the cost both of repairs and hydrogen gas is taken into count.

(*c*) When the wind is against one — as it was on this occasion — one finds less of it in these low altitudes.

So I guide roped up the Avenue of the Bois. So, someday, will explorers guide rope to the North Pole from their ice-locked steamship after it has reached its farthest possible point north. Guide roping over the ice pack, they will make the very few hundreds of miles to the Pole at the rate of from 60 to 80 kilometers (40 to 50 miles) per hour. Even at the rate of 50 kilometers (30 miles), the trip to the Pole and back to the ship could be taken between breakfast and supper time. I do not say that they will land the first time at the Pole, but they will circle round about the spot, take observations, and return — for supper!

I might have guide roped under the Arc de Triomphe had I thought myself worthy. Instead, I rounded the national monument, to the right, as the law directs. Naturally, I had intended to go on straight down the Avenue des Champs Élysées; but here I met a difficulty. All the avenues meeting at the great "Star" look alike from the airship. Also, they look narrow. I was surprised and confused for a moment, and it was only by looking back, to note the situation of the arch, that I could find my avenue.

Like that of the Bois, it was deserted. Far down its length I saw a solitary cab. As I guide roped along it to my house at the corner of the Rue Washington, I thought of the time, sure to come, when the owners of handy little airships will not be obliged to land in the street, but will have their guide ropes caught by their domestics on their own roof gardens. But such roof gardens must be broad and unincumbered.

So I reached my corner, to which I pointed my stem slightly and descended very gently. Two servants caught, steadied, and held the airship while I mounted to my apartment for a cup of coffee. From my round bay window at the corner I looked down upon the airship. Were I to receive the municipal permission, it would not be difficult to build an ornamental landing stage out from that window!

Projects like these will constitute work for the future. Meanwhile the aerial idea is making progress. A small boy of seven years of age has mounted with me in the "No. 9," and a charming young lady has actually navigated it alone for something like a mile! The boy will surely make an airship captain, if he gives his mind to it. The occasion was the Children's Fête at Bagatelle, on June 26, 1903. Descending among them in the "No. 9," I asked:

"Does any little boy want to go up?"

Such were the confidence and courage of young France and America, that instantly I had to choose among a dozen volunteers. I took the nearest to me.

"Are you not afraid?" I asked as the airship rose.

"Not a bit!" he answered. The cruise of the "No. 9" on this occasion was naturally a short one; but the other, in which the first woman to mount, accompanied or unaccompanied, in any airship, actually mounted alone and drove the "No. 9" free from all human contact with its guide rope for a distance of considerably over a half mile, is worthy of preservation in the annals of aerial navigation.

The heroine, a very beautiful young lady well known in New York society, having visited my station with her friends on several occasions, confessed an extraordinary desire to navigate the airship.

"You mean that you would have the courage to be taken up in the free balloon, with no one holding its guide rope?" I asked. "Mademoiselle, I thank you for the confidence!"

"Oh, no," she said. "I do not want to be taken up. I want to go up alone and navigate it free, as you do."

I think that the simple fact that I consented on condition that she would take a few lessons in the handling of the motor and machinery speaks eloquently in favor of my own confidence in the "No. 9." She had three such lessons, and then on June 29, 1903, a date that will be memorable in the Fasti of dirigible ballooning, rising from my station grounds in the smallest of possible dirigibles, she cried: "Let go, all!"

From my station at Neuilly Saint James she guide roped to Bagatelle. The guide rope trailing some 30 feet gave her an altitude and equilibrium that never varied. I will not say that no one ran along beside the dragging guide rope, but, certainly, no one touched it until the termination of the cruise at Bagatelle, when the moment had arrived to pull down the intrepid girl navigator.

CHAPTER XXIII

THE AIRSHIP IN WAR

On Saturday, July 11, 1903, at about 10 A.M., the wind blowing at the time in gusts, I accepted a wager to go to luncheon at the sylvan restaurant of "The Cascade" in my little "No. 9" airship. While the "No. 9," with its egg-shaped balloon and motor of but 3 horsepower, is not built for speed — or, what amounts to the same thing, for battling with the wind — I thought that I could do it. Reaching my station at Neuilly Saint James at about 11:30 A.M., I had the little craft brought out and carefully weighed and balanced. It was in perfect condition, having lost none of its gas from the previous day. At 11:50 I started off. Fortunately, the wind came to me head-on as I steered for "The Cascade." My progress was not rapid, but I, nevertheless, met my friends on the lawn of that famous restaurant of the Bois de Boulogne at 12:30 noon. We took our luncheon, and I was preparing to depart when there began an adventure that may take me far.

As everybody knows, the restaurant of "The Cascade" is close to Longchamps. While we lunched, officers of the French army engaged in marking out the positions of the troops for the grand review of July 14 observed the airship on the lawn, and came to inspect it.

"Shall you come to the review in it?" they asked me. The year previous there had been question of such a demonstration in presence of the army, but I had hesitated for reasons that may be readily divined. After the visit of the King of England, I was asked on every hand why I had not brought out the airship in his honor, and the same questions had arisen in anticipation of the visit of the King of Italy, who had been expected to be present at this review.

I answered the officers that I could not make up my mind; that I was not sure how such an apparition would be viewed; and that my little "No. 9," — the only one of my fleet actually "in commission," — not being built for battling with high winds, I could not be sure to keep an engagement in it.

"Come and choose a place to land," they said; "we will mark it out for you, in any case." And, as I continued to insist on my uncertainty of being present, they very courteously picked out and marked a place for me themselves, opposite the spot to be occupied by the President of the Republic, in order that M. Loubet and his staff might have a perfect view of the airship's evolutions.

"You will come if you can," the officers said. "You need not fear to make such a provisional engagement, for you have already given your proofs."

I hope I shall not be misunderstood when I say that it may be possible that those superior officers did good work for their army and country that morning because, in order to begin, one must make a beginning; and I should scarcely have ventured to the review without some kind of invitation.

As a consequence of my visit a whole train of events followed.

In the early morning of July 14, 1903, as the "No. 9" was weighed and balanced, I was nervous lest some unforeseen thing might happen to it in my very grounds. One is often thus on great occasions, and I did not seek to conceal it from myself that this, the first presentation of an airship to any army, would be a great occasion.

On ordinary days I never hesitate to mount from my grounds, over the stone wall and the river, and so on to Bagatelle. This morning I had the "No. 9" towed to the railing of Bagatelle by means of its guide rope.

At 8:30 A.M. I called, "Let go, all!" Rising, I found my level course at an altitude of less than 350 feet, and in a few moments was circling and maneuvering above the heads of the soldiers nearest to me. Thence I passed over Longchamps, and arriving opposite the President, I fired a salute of twenty-one blank revolver cartridges.

I did not take the place marked out for me. Fearing to disturb the good order of the review by prolonging an unusual sight, I made my evolutions in the presence of the army last, all told, less than ten minutes. After this I steered for the Polo Grounds, where I was congratulated by numbers of my friends.

These congratulations I found the next day repeated in the Paris papers, together with conjectures of all kinds concerning the use

43.   The "Santos-Dumont No. 9," the little runabout

44. The "Santos-Dumont No. 9" at military review, July 14, 1903

of the airship in war. The superior officers who came to me at "The Cascade" that morning had said: "It is practical, and will have to be taken account of in war."

"I am entirely at your service," had been my answer at the time; and now, under these influences, I sat down and wrote to the Minister of War, offering, in case of hostilities with any country save those of the two Americas, to put my aerial fleet at the disposition of the government of the Republic.

In doing this I merely put into formal written words the offer which I certainly should feel bound to make in case of the breaking out of such hostilities at any future time during my residence in France. It is in France that I have met with all my encouragement; in France and with French material I have made all my experiments; and the mass of my friends are French. I excepted the two Americas because I am an American, and I added that in the impossible case of a war between France and Brazil, I should feel bound to volunteer my services to the land of my birth and citizenship.

A few days later I received the following letter from the French Minister of War:

MINISTÈRE DE LA GUERRE,
Cabinet du Ministre,
République Française,
Paris, le 19 juillet, 1903

MONSIEUR:

During the review of July 14, I had remarked and admired the ease and security with which the balloon you were steering made its evolutions. It was impossible not to acknowledge the progress which you have given to aerial navigation. It seems that, thanks to you, such navigation must henceforward lend itself to practical applications, especially from the military point of view.

I consider that, in this respect, it may render very substantial services in time of war. I am very happy, therefore, to accept the offer which you make, of putting, in case of need, your aerial flotilla at the disposition of the government of the Republic, and, in its name, I thank you for your gracious proposition, which shows your lively sympathy for France.

I have appointed Chief of Battalion Hirschauer, commanding the Battalion of Balloonists in the First Regiment of Engineers, to examine, in agreement with you, the dispositions to take for putting the intentions you have manifested into execution. Lieutenant Colonel

Bourdeaux, Sous-Chef of my Cabinet, will also be associated with this superior officer, in order to keep me personally aware of the results of your joint labors.

Recevez, Monsieur, les assurances de ma consideration la plus distinguée.

GÉNÉRAL ANDRÉ
À Monsieur Alberto Santos-Dumont.

On Friday, July 31, 1903, Commandant Hirschauer and Lieutenant Colonel Bourdeaux spent the afternoon with me at my airship station at Neuilly Saint James, where I had my three newest airships, the racing "No. 7," the omnibus "No. 10," and the runabout "No. 9," ready for their study. Briefly, I may say that the opinions expressed by the representatives of the Minister of War were so unreservedly favorable that a practical test of a novel character was decided to be made. Should the airship chosen pass successfully through it, the result will be conclusive of its military value.

Now that these particular experiments are leaving my exclusively private control, I will say no more of them than what has been already published in the French press. The test will probably consist of an attempt to enter one of the French frontier towns, such as Belfort or Nancy, on the same day that the airship leaves Paris. It will not, of course, be necessary to make the whole journey in the airship. A military railway wagon may be assigned to carry it, with its balloon uninflated, with tubes of hydrogen to fill it, and with all the necessary machinery and instruments arranged beside it. At some station a short distance from the town to be entered, the wagon may be uncoupled from the train, and a sufficient number of soldiers accompanying the officers will unload the airship and its appliances, transport the whole to the nearest open space, and at once begin inflating the balloon. Within two hours from the time of quitting the train, the airship may be ready for its flight to the interior of the technically besieged town.

Such may be the outline of the task — a task presented imperiously to French balloonists by the events of 1870-71, and which all the devotion and science of the Tissandier brothers failed to accomplish. Today, the problem may be set with better hope of success. All the essential difficulties may be revived by the marking out of a hostile zone around the town that must be entered; from beyond the outer edge of this zone, then, the airship will rise and take its flight — across it.

Will the airship be able to rise out of rifle range? I have always been the first to insist that the normal place of the airship is in low altitudes, and I shall have written this book to little purpose if I have not shown the reader the real dangers attending any brusque vertical mounting to considerable heights. For this we have the terrible Severo accident before our eyes. In particular, I have expressed astonishment at hearing of experimenters rising to these altitudes without adequate purpose in their early stages of experience with dirigible balloons. All this is very different, however, from a reasoned, cautious mounting, whose necessity has been foreseen and prepared for.

To keep out of rifle range, the airship will but seldom be obliged to make these tremendous vertical leaps. Its navigator, even at a moderate altitude, will enjoy a very extended view of the surrounding country. Thus he will be able to perceive danger afar off and take his precautions. Even in my little "No. 9," which carries only 60 kilograms (132 pounds) of ballast, I could rise — materially aided by my shifting weights and propeller — to great heights. If I have not done so, it is because it would have served no useful purpose during a period of pleasure navigation, while it would but have added danger to experiments from which I have sought to eliminate all danger. Hazards like these are to be accepted only when a good cause justifies them.

The experiments above named are, of course, of a nature interesting warfare by land. I cannot abandon this topic, however, without referring to one unique maritime advantage of the airship. This is its navigator's ability to perceive bodies moving beneath the surface of the water. Cruising at the end of its guide rope, the airship will carry its navigator here and there at will, at the right height above the waves. Any submarine boat, stealthily pursuing its course underneath them, will be beautifully visible to him, while from a warship's deck it would be quite invisible. This is a well-observed fact, and depends on certain optical laws. Thus, very curiously, the twentieth-century airship must become, from the beginning, the great enemy of that other twentieth-century marvel, the submarine boat! And not only its enemy, but its master! For, while the submarine boat can do no harm to the airship, the latter, having twice its speed, can cruise about to find it, follow all its movements, and signal them to the warships against which it is moving. Indeed, it may be able to destroy the submarine boat by sending down to it long arrows filled with dynamite and capable of penetrating to depths underneath the waves impossible to gunnery from the decks of a warship!

CHAPTER XXIV

PARIS AS A CENTER OF AIRSHIP EXPERIMENTS

After leaving Monte Carlo in February, 1902, I received many invitations from abroad to navigate my airships. In London, in particular, I was received with great friendliness by the Aéro Club of Great Britain, under whose auspices my "No. 6," fished from the bottom of the Bay of Monaco, repaired, and once again inflated, was exhibited at the Crystal Palace.

From St. Louis, where the organizers of the Louisiana Purchase Centennial Exposition had already decided to make airship flights a feature of their World's Fair in 1904, I received an invitation to inspect the grounds, suggest a course, and confer with them on conditions. As it was officially announced that a sum of $200,000 had been voted and set apart for prizes, it might be expected that the emulation of airship experimenters would be well aroused.

Arriving at St. Louis in the summer of 1902, I at once saw that the splendid open spaces of the exposition grounds offered the best of racecourses. The prevailing idea at that moment in the minds of some of the authorities was to set a long course of many hundreds of miles — say from St. Louis to Chicago. This, I pointed out, would be unpractical, if only for the reason that the exposition public would desire to see the flights from start to finish. I suggested that three great towers or flagstaffs be erected in the grounds at the corners of an equal-sided triangle. The comparatively short course around them — between ten and twenty miles — would afford a decisive test of dirigibility, no matter in what way the wind might blow; while as for speed, the necessary average might be increased fifty per cent over that fixed for the Deutsch Prize competition in Paris.

Such was my modest advice. I also thought that, out of the appropriation of $200,000, a grand prize for dirigible aerostation of $100,000 should be offered; only by means of such an inducement, it seemed to me, could the necessary emulation among airship experimenters be aroused.

While never seeking to make profit from my airships, I have always offered to compete for prizes. While in London, and again in New York, both before and after my St. Louis visit, competitions with prize sanctions were suggested to me for immediate effort. I accepted all of them to this point, that I had my airships brought to the spot at considerable cost and effort, and had the prize funds been deposited, I would have done my best to win them. Such deposits failing, I in each case returned to my home in Paris, to continue my experiments in my own way, awaiting the great competition of St. Louis.

Prize or no prize, I must work, and I shall always work in this my chosen field of aerostation. For this my place is Paris, where the public, in particular the kindly and enthusiastic populace, both knows and trusts me. Here in Paris I go up for my own pleasure, day by day, as my reward for long and costly experiment.

In England and America it is quite different. When I take my airships and my employees to those countries, build my own balloon house, furnish my own gas plant, and risk breaking machines that cost more than any automobile, I want it to be done with a settled aim.

I say that I want it to be done with a settled aim so that, if I fulfil the aim, I may no longer be criticized, at least on that particular head. Otherwise I might go to the moon and back and yet accomplish nothing in the estimation of my critics, and — though perhaps to a less extent — in the mind of the public which they seek to sway.

Here is the principal reason why I have sought to win prizes: because the most rational consecration of such effort and its fulfilment is found in a serious money prize. The mind of the public makes the obvious connection. When a valuable prize is handed over, it concludes that something has been done to win it.

45. Guide roping over the housetops

46. Guide roping lower than the housetops

To win such prizes, then, I waited long in London and New York; but, as they never passed from words to deeds, after having enjoyed myself very thoroughly both socially and as a tourist, I returned to my work and pleasure in the Paris which I call my home.

And, really, after all is said and done, there is no place like Paris for airship experiments. Nowhere else can the experimenter depend on the municipal and state authorities to be so liberal.

Take the development of automobilism as an example. It is universally admitted, I imagine, that this great and peculiarly French industry could not have developed without the speed license which the French authorities have wide mindedly permitted. In spite of the most powerful social and industrial influences, and in spite of it being England's turn to offer hospitality to the James Gordon Bennett Cup Race of 1903, the English automobilists were not allowed to put their splendid roads out of the public use for its accommodation for a single day. So the great event had to come off in Ireland.

In France, and in France only, are not only the authorities, but the great mass of citizens, so much alive to their advantage in the development of this national industry that, day by day, year in and year out, they permit ten thousand automobiles to go tearing through their highroads at a really dangerous speed. In Paris, in particular, one sees a "scorching" average in its great park, and in its very avenues and streets, that causes Londoners and tourists from New York to stand aghast.

In this same order of ideas I may here state that, in spite of the tragic airship accidents of 1902, I have never once been limited or in any way impeded in the course of my experiments by the Parisian authorities; while, as for the public, no matter where I land with an airship — in the country roads of the suburbs, in private gardens even of great villas, in the avenues and parks and public places of the capital — I meet with unvarying friendly aid, protection, and enthusiasm from the crowd!

From that first memorable day when the big boys flying their kites over Bagatelle seized my guide rope and saved me from an ugly fall as promptly and intelligently as they had seized the idea of pulling me against the wind, to the critical moment on that summer day in 1901 when, in my first trial for the Deutsch Prize, I descended to repair my rudder and good-natured workingmen found me a ladder in less time than it takes me to write the words, and on down to the present moment when I take my pleasure in the Bois in my small "No. 9," I have had nothing but unvarying friendliness from the intelligent Parisian populace.

I need not say that it is a great thing for an airship experimenter thus to have the confidence and friendly aid of a whole population. Over certain European frontiers spherical balloons have even been shot at! And I have often wondered what kind of a reception one of my airships would meet with in the country districts of England itself.

For these reasons and a hundred others, I consider that my airship's home, like my own, is Paris. As a boy in Brazil, my heart turned to the City of Light, above which, in 1783, the first Montgolfier had been sent up; where the first of the world's aeronauts had made his first ascension; where the first hydrogen balloon had been set loose; where first an airship had been made to navigate the air with its steam engine, screw propeller, and rudder.

As a youth I made my own first balloon ascension from Paris. In Paris I have found balloon constructors, motor makers, and machinists possessed not only of skill but of patience. In Paris I made all my first experiments. In Paris I won the Deutsch Prize in the first dirigible to do a task against a time limit. And now that I have not only what I call my racing airship, but a little "runabout," in which to take my pleasure over the trees of the Bois, it is in Paris that I am enjoying my reward in it as — what I was once called reproachfully — an "aerostatic sportsman"!

MORE REASONING OF CHILDREN

During these years Luis and Pedro, the ingenuous country boys whom we found reasoning about mechanical inventions in the introductory fable of this book, have spent some time in Paris. They were present at the winning of the Deutsch Prize for aerial navigation; they spent the winter of 1901-1902 at Monte Carlo; they had good places at the review of July 14, 1903; and they have broadened their education by the sedulous reading of scientific weeklies and the daily newspapers. Now they are preparing to return to Brazil.

The other day, seated on the terrace of the Cascade in the Bois de Boulogne, they argued on the problem of aerial navigation.

"These tentatives with so-called dirigible balloons can bring us no nearer to its solution," said Pedro. "Look you, they are filled with a substance — hydrogen — fourteen times lighter than the medium in which it floats — the atmosphere. It would be just as possible to force a tallow candle through a brick wall!"

"Pedro," said Luis, "do you remember your objections to my wagon wheels?"

.   .   .   .

"To the locomotive engine?"

.   .   .   .

"To the steamboat?"

.   .   .   .   .   .

"Our only hope to navigate the air," continued Pedro, taking no notice of these interrogations, "must, in the nature of things, be found in devices heavier than the air, in flying-machines or aeroplanes. Reason by analogy. Look at the bird. . . ."

"Once you desired me to look at the fish," said Luis. "You said the steamboat ought to wriggle through the water. . . ."

"Do be serious, Luis," said Pedro, in conclusive tones. "Exercise common sense. Does man fly? No. Does the bird fly? Yes. Then, if man would fly, let him imitate the bird. Nature has made the bird. Nature never goes wrong."

A CATALOGUE OF SELECTED DOVER BOOKS
IN ALL FIELDS OF INTEREST

A CATALOGUE OF SELECTED DOVER BOOKS
IN ALL FIELDS OF INTEREST

AMERICA'S OLD MASTERS, James T. Flexner. Four men emerged unexpectedly from provincial 18th century America to leadership in European art: Benjamin West, J. S. Copley, C. R. Peale, Gilbert Stuart. Brilliant coverage of lives and contributions. Revised, 1967 edition. 69 plates. 365pp. of text.
21806-6 Paperbound $3.00

FIRST FLOWERS OF OUR WILDERNESS: AMERICAN PAINTING, THE COLONIAL PERIOD, James T. Flexner. Painters, and regional painting traditions from earliest Colonial times up to the emergence of Copley, West and Peale Sr., Foster, Gustavus Hesselius, Feke, John Smibert and many anonymous painters in the primitive manner. Engaging presentation, with 162 illustrations. xxii + 368pp.
22180-6 Paperbound $3.50

THE LIGHT OF DISTANT SKIES: AMERICAN PAINTING, 1760-1835, James T. Flexner. The great generation of early American painters goes to Europe to learn and to teach: West, Copley, Gilbert Stuart and others. Allston, Trumbull, Morse; also contemporary American painters—primitives, derivatives, academics—who remained in America. 102 illustrations. xiii + 306pp.
22179-2 Paperbound $3.50

A HISTORY OF THE RISE AND PROGRESS OF THE ARTS OF DESIGN IN THE UNITED STATES, William Dunlap. Much the richest mine of information on early American painters, sculptors, architects, engravers, miniaturists, etc. The only source of information for scores of artists, the major primary source for many others. Unabridged reprint of rare original 1834 edition, with new introduction by James T. Flexner, and 394 new illustrations. Edited by Rita Weiss. 6⅝ x 9⅜.
21695-0, 21696-9, 21697-7 Three volumes, Paperbound $13.50

EPOCHS OF CHINESE AND JAPANESE ART, Ernest F. Fenollosa. From primitive Chinese art to the 20th century, thorough history, explanation of every important art period and form, including Japanese woodcuts; main stress on China and Japan, but Tibet, Korea also included. Still unexcelled for its detailed, rich coverage of cultural background, aesthetic elements, diffusion studies, particularly of the historical period. 2nd, 1913 edition. 242 illustrations. lii + 439pp. of text.
20364-6, 20365-4 Two volumes, Paperbound $6.00

THE GENTLE ART OF MAKING ENEMIES, James A. M. Whistler. Greatest wit of his day deflates Oscar Wilde, Ruskin, Swinburne; strikes back at inane critics, exhibitions, art journalism; aesthetics of impressionist revolution in most striking form. Highly readable classic by great painter. Reproduction of edition designed by Whistler. Introduction by Alfred Werner. xxxvi + 334pp.
21875-9 Paperbound $2.50

VISUAL ILLUSIONS: THEIR CAUSES, CHARACTERISTICS, AND APPLICATIONS, Matthew Luckiesh. Thorough description and discussion of optical illusion, geometric and perspective, particularly; size and shape distortions, illusions of color, of motion; natural illusions; use of illusion in art and magic, industry, etc. Most useful today with op art, also for classical art. Scores of effects illustrated. Introduction by William H. Ittleson. 100 illustrations. xxi + 252pp.
21530-X Paperbound $2.00

A HANDBOOK OF ANATOMY FOR ART STUDENTS, Arthur Thomson. Thorough, virtually exhaustive coverage of skeletal structure, musculature, etc. Full text, supplemented by anatomical diagrams and drawings and by photographs of undraped figures. Unique in its comparison of male and female forms, pointing out differences of contour, texture, form. 211 figures, 40 drawings, 86 photographs. xx + 459pp. 5⅜ x 8⅜.
21163-0 Paperbound $3.50

150 MASTERPIECES OF DRAWING, Selected by Anthony Toney. Full page reproductions of drawings from the early 16th to the end of the 18th century, all beautifully reproduced: Rembrandt, Michelangelo, Dürer, Fragonard, Urs, Graf, Wouwerman, many others. First-rate browsing book, model book for artists. xviii + 150pp. 8⅜ x 11¼.
21032-4 Paperbound $2.50

THE LATER WORK OF AUBREY BEARDSLEY, Aubrey Beardsley. Exotic, erotic, ironic masterpieces in full maturity: Comedy Ballet, Venus and Tannhauser, Pierrot, Lysistrata, Rape of the Lock, Savoy material, Ali Baba, Volpone, etc. This material revolutionized the art world, and is still powerful, fresh, brilliant. With *The Early Work*, all Beardsley's finest work. 174 plates, 2 in color. xiv + 176pp. 8⅛ x 11.
21817-1 Paperbound $3.00

DRAWINGS OF REMBRANDT, Rembrandt van Rijn. Complete reproduction of fabulously rare edition by Lippmann and Hofstede de Groot, completely reedited, updated, improved by Prof. Seymour Slive, Fogg Museum. Portraits, Biblical sketches, landscapes, Oriental types, nudes, episodes from classical mythology—All Rembrandt's fertile genius. Also selection of drawings by his pupils and followers. "Stunning volumes," *Saturday Review*. 550 illustrations. lxxviii + 552pp. 9⅛ x 12¼.
21485-0, 21486-9 Two volumes, Paperbound $10.00

THE DISASTERS OF WAR, Francisco Goya. One of the masterpieces of Western civilization—83 etchings that record Goya's shattering, bitter reaction to the Napoleonic war that swept through Spain after the insurrection of 1808 and to war in general. Reprint of the first edition, with three additional plates from Boston's Museum of Fine Arts. All plates facsimile size. Introduction by Philip Hofer, Fogg Museum. v + 97pp. 9⅜ x 8¼.
21872-4 Paperbound $2.00

GRAPHIC WORKS OF ODILON REDON. Largest collection of Redon's graphic works ever assembled: 172 lithographs, 28 etchings and engravings, 9 drawings. These include some of his most famous works. All the plates from *Odilon Redon: oeuvre graphique complet,* plus additional plates. New introduction and caption translations by Alfred Werner. 209 illustrations. xxvii + 209pp. 9⅛ x 12¼.
21966-8 Paperbound $4.00

DESIGN BY ACCIDENT; A BOOK OF "ACCIDENTAL EFFECTS" FOR ARTISTS AND DESIGNERS, James F. O'Brien. Create your own unique, striking, imaginative effects by "controlled accident" interaction of materials: paints and lacquers, oil and water based paints, splatter, crackling materials, shatter, similar items. Everything you do will be different; first book on this limitless art, so useful to both fine artist and commercial artist. Full instructions. 192 plates showing "accidents," 8 in color. viii + 215pp. 8⅜ x 11¼. 21942-9 Paperbound $3.50

THE BOOK OF SIGNS, Rudolf Koch. Famed German type designer draws 493 beautiful symbols: religious, mystical, alchemical, imperial, property marks, runes, etc. Remarkable fusion of traditional and modern. Good for suggestions of timelessness, smartness, modernity. Text. vi + 104pp. 6⅛ x 9¼. 20162-7 Paperbound $1.25

HISTORY OF INDIAN AND INDONESIAN ART, Ananda K. Coomaraswamy. An unabridged republication of one of the finest books by a great scholar in Eastern art. Rich in descriptive material, history, social backgrounds; Sunga reliefs, Rajput paintings, Gupta temples, Burmese frescoes, textiles, jewelry, sculpture, etc. 400 photos. viii + 423pp. 6⅜ x 9¾. 21436-2 Paperbound $5.00

PRIMITIVE ART, Franz Boas. America's foremost anthropologist surveys textiles, ceramics, woodcarving, basketry, metalwork, etc.; patterns, technology, creation of symbols, style origins. All areas of world, but very full on Northwest Coast Indians. More than 350 illustrations of baskets, boxes, totem poles, weapons, etc. 378 pp. 20025-6 Paperbound $3.00

THE GENTLEMAN AND CABINET MAKER'S DIRECTOR, Thomas Chippendale. Full reprint (third edition, 1762) of most influential furniture book of all time, by master cabinetmaker. 200 plates, illustrating chairs, sofas, mirrors, tables, cabinets, plus 24 photographs of surviving pieces. Biographical introduction by N. Bienenstock. vi + 249pp. 9⅞ x 12¾. 21601-2 Paperbound $4.00

AMERICAN ANTIQUE FURNITURE, Edgar G. Miller, Jr. The basic coverage of all American furniture before 1840. Individual chapters cover type of furniture—clocks, tables, sideboards, etc.—chronologically, with inexhaustible wealth of data. More than 2100 photographs, all identified, commented on. Essential to all early American collectors. Introduction by H. E. Keyes. vi + 1106pp. 7⅞ x 10¾. 21599-7, 21600-4 Two volumes, Paperbound $11.00

PENNSYLVANIA DUTCH AMERICAN FOLK ART, Henry J. Kauffman. 279 photos, 28 drawings of tulipware, Fraktur script, painted tinware, toys, flowered furniture, quilts, samplers, hex signs, house interiors, etc. Full descriptive text. Excellent for tourist, rewarding for designer, collector. Map. 146pp. 7⅞ x 10¾. 21205-X Paperbound $2.50

EARLY NEW ENGLAND GRAVESTONE RUBBINGS, Edmund V. Gillon, Jr. 43 photographs, 226 carefully reproduced rubbings show heavily symbolic, sometimes macabre early gravestones, up to early 19th century. Remarkable early American primitive art, occasionally strikingly beautiful; always powerful. Text. xxvi + 207pp. 8⅜ x 11¼. 21380-3 Paperbound $3.50

ALPHABETS AND ORNAMENTS, Ernst Lehner. Well-known pictorial source for decorative alphabets, script examples, cartouches, frames, decorative title pages, calligraphic initials, borders, similar material. 14th to 19th century, mostly European. Useful in almost any graphic arts designing, varied styles. 750 illustrations. 256pp. 7 x 10. 21905-4 Paperbound $4.00

PAINTING: A CREATIVE APPROACH, Norman Colquhoun. For the beginner simple guide provides an instructive approach to painting: major stumbling blocks for beginner; overcoming them, technical points; paints and pigments; oil painting; watercolor and other media and color. New section on "plastic" paints. Glossary. Formerly *Paint Your Own Pictures*. 221pp. 22000-1 Paperbound $1.75

THE ENJOYMENT AND USE OF COLOR, Walter Sargent. Explanation of the relations between colors themselves and between colors in nature and art, including hundreds of little-known facts about color values, intensities, effects of high and low illumination, complementary colors. Many practical hints for painters, references to great masters. 7 color plates, 29 illustrations. x + 274pp.
20944-X Paperbound $2.75

THE NOTEBOOKS OF LEONARDO DA VINCI, compiled and edited by Jean Paul Richter. 1566 extracts from original manuscripts reveal the full range of Leonardo's versatile genius: all his writings on painting, sculpture, architecture, anatomy, astronomy, geography, topography, physiology, mining, music, etc., in both Italian and English, with 186 plates of manuscript pages and more than 500 additional drawings. Includes studies for the Last Supper, the lost Sforza monument, and other works. Total of xlvii + 866pp. 7⅞ x 10¾.
22572-0, 22573-9 Two volumes, Paperbound $10.00

MONTGOMERY WARD CATALOGUE OF 1895. Tea gowns, yards of flannel and pillow-case lace, stereoscopes, books of gospel hymns, the New Improved Singer Sewing Machine, side saddles, milk skimmers, straight-edged razors, high-button shoes, spittoons, and on and on . . . listing some 25,000 items, practically all illustrated. Essential to the shoppers of the 1890's, it is our truest record of the spirit of the period. Unaltered reprint of Issue No. 57, Spring and Summer 1895. Introduction by Boris Emmet. Innumerable illustrations. xiii + 624pp. 8½ x 11⅝.
22377-9 Paperbound $6.95

THE CRYSTAL PALACE EXHIBITION ILLUSTRATED CATALOGUE (LONDON, 1851). One of the wonders of the modern world—the Crystal Palace Exhibition in which all the nations of the civilized world exhibited their achievements in the arts and sciences—presented in an equally important illustrated catalogue. More than 1700 items pictured with accompanying text—ceramics, textiles, cast-iron work, carpets, pianos, sleds, razors, wall-papers, billiard tables, beehives, silverware and hundreds of other artifacts—represent the focal point of Victorian culture in the Western World. Probably the largest collection of Victorian decorative art ever assembled—indispensable for antiquarians and designers. Unabridged republication of the Art-Journal Catalogue of the Great Exhibition of 1851, with all terminal essays. New introduction by John Gloag, F.S.A. xxxiv + 426pp. 9 x 12.
22503-8 Paperbound $4.50

A HISTORY OF COSTUME, Carl Köhler. Definitive history, based on surviving pieces of clothing primarily, and paintings, statues, etc. secondarily. Highly readable text, supplemented by 594 illustrations of costumes of the ancient Mediterranean peoples, Greece and Rome, the Teutonic prehistoric period; costumes of the Middle Ages, Renaissance, Baroque, 18th and 19th centuries. Clear, measured patterns are provided for many clothing articles. Approach is practical throughout. Enlarged by Emma von Sichart. 464pp.　　　　　　　　　　21030-8 Paperbound $3.50

ORIENTAL RUGS, ANTIQUE AND MODERN, Walter A. Hawley. A complete and authoritative treatise on the Oriental rug—where they are made, by whom and how, designs and symbols, characteristics in detail of the six major groups, how to distinguish them and how to buy them. Detailed technical data is provided on periods, weaves, warps, wefts, textures, sides, ends and knots, although no technical background is required for an understanding. 11 color plates, 80 halftones, 4 maps. vi + 320pp. 6⅛ x 9⅛.　　　　　　　　　　22366-3 Paperbound $5.00

TEN BOOKS ON ARCHITECTURE, Vitruvius. By any standards the most important book on architecture ever written. Early Roman discussion of aesthetics of building, construction methods, orders, sites, and every other aspect of architecture has inspired, instructed architecture for about 2,000 years. Stands behind Palladio, Michelangelo, Bramante, Wren, countless others. Definitive Morris H. Morgan translation. 68 illustrations. xii + 331pp.　　　　　　20645-9 Paperbound $3.00

THE FOUR BOOKS OF ARCHITECTURE, Andrea Palladio. Translated into every major Western European language in the two centuries following its publication in 1570, this has been one of the most influential books in the history of architecture. Complete reprint of the 1738 Isaac Ware edition. New introduction by Adolf Placzek, Columbia Univ. 216 plates. xxii + 110pp. of text. 9½ x 12¾.
21308-0 Clothbound $10.00

STICKS AND STONES: A STUDY OF AMERICAN ARCHITECTURE AND CIVILIZATION, Lewis Mumford.One of the great classics of American cultural history. American architecture from the medieval-inspired earliest forms to the early 20th century; evolution of structure and style, and reciprocal influences on environment. 21 photographic illustrations. 238pp.　　　　　　　　　20202-X Paperbound $2.00

THE AMERICAN BUILDER'S COMPANION, Asher Benjamin. The most widely used early 19th century architectural style and source book, for colonial up into Greek Revival periods. Extensive development of geometry of carpentering, construction of sashes, frames, doors, stairs; plans and elevations of domestic and other buildings. Hundreds of thousands of houses were built according to this book, now invaluable to historians, architects, restorers, etc. 1827 edition. 59 plates. 114pp. 7⅞ x 10¾.
22236-5 Paperbound $3.50

DUTCH HOUSES IN THE HUDSON VALLEY BEFORE 1776, Helen Wilkinson Reynolds. The standard survey of the Dutch colonial house and outbuildings, with constructional features, decoration, and local history associated with individual homesteads. Introduction by Franklin D. Roosevelt. Map. 150 illustrations. 469pp. 6⅝ x 9¼.　　　　　　　　　　　　　　21469-9 Paperbound $4.00

THE ARCHITECTURE OF COUNTRY HOUSES, Andrew J. Downing. Together with Vaux's *Villas and Cottages* this is the basic book for Hudson River Gothic architecture of the middle Victorian period. Full, sound discussions of general aspects of housing, architecture, style, decoration, furnishing, together with scores of detailed house plans, illustrations of specific buildings, accompanied by full text. Perhaps the most influential single American architectural book. 1850 edition. Introduction by J. Stewart Johnson. 321 figures, 34 architectural designs. xvi + 560pp.

22003-6 Paperbound $4.00

LOST EXAMPLES OF COLONIAL ARCHITECTURE, John Mead Howells. Full-page photographs of buildings that have disappeared or been so altered as to be denatured, including many designed by major early American architects. 245 plates. xvii + 248pp. 7⅞ x 10¾.

21143-6 Paperbound $3.50

DOMESTIC ARCHITECTURE OF THE AMERICAN COLONIES AND OF THE EARLY REPUBLIC, Fiske Kimball. Foremost architect and restorer of Williamsburg and Monticello covers nearly 200 homes between 1620-1825. Architectural details, construction, style features, special fixtures, floor plans, etc. Generally considered finest work in its area. 219 illustrations of houses, doorways, windows, capital mantels. xx + 314pp. 7⅞ x 10¾.

21743-4 Paperbound $4.00

EARLY AMERICAN ROOMS: 1650-1858, edited by Russell Hawes Kettell. Tour of 12 rooms, each representative of a different era in American history and each furnished, decorated, designed and occupied in the style of the era. 72 plans and elevations, 8-page color section, etc., show fabrics, wall papers, arrangements, etc. Full descriptive text. xvii + 200pp. of text. 8⅜ x 11¼.

21633-0 Paperbound $5.00

THE FITZWILLIAM VIRGINAL BOOK, edited by J. Fuller Maitland and W. B. Squire. Full modern printing of famous early 17th-century ms. volume of 300 works by Morley, Byrd, Bull, Gibbons, etc. For piano or other modern keyboard instrument; easy to read format. xxxvi + 938pp. 8⅜ x 11.

21068-5, 21069-3 Two volumes, Paperbound $10.00

KEYBOARD MUSIC, Johann Sebastian Bach. Bach Gesellschaft edition. A rich selection of Bach's masterpieces for the harpsichord: the six English Suites, six French Suites, the six Partitas (Clavierübung part I), the Goldberg Variations (Clavierübung part IV), the fifteen Two-Part Inventions and the fifteen Three-Part Sinfonias. Clearly reproduced on large sheets with ample margins; eminently playable. vi + 312pp. 8⅛ x 11.

22360-4 Paperbound $5.00

THE MUSIC OF BACH: AN INTRODUCTION, Charles Sanford Terry. A fine, non-technical introduction to Bach's music, both instrumental and vocal. Covers organ music, chamber music, passion music, other types. Analyzes themes, developments, innovations. x + 114pp.

21075-8 Paperbound $1.25

BEETHOVEN AND HIS NINE SYMPHONIES, Sir George Grove. Noted British musicologist provides best history, analysis, commentary on symphonies. Very thorough, rigorously accurate; necessary to both advanced student and amateur music lover. 436 musical passages. vii + 407 pp.

20334-4 Paperbound $2.75

JOHANN SEBASTIAN BACH, Philipp Spitta. One of the great classics of musicology, this definitive analysis of Bach's music (and life) has never been surpassed. Lucid, nontechnical analyses of hundreds of pieces (30 pages devoted to St. Matthew Passion, 26 to B Minor Mass). Also includes major analysis of 18th-century music. 450 musical examples. 40-page musical supplement. Total of xx + 1799pp.
(EUK) 22278-0, 22279-9 Two volumes, Clothbound $17.50

MOZART AND HIS PIANO CONCERTOS, Cuthbert Girdlestone. The only full-length study of an important area of Mozart's creativity. Provides detailed analyses of all 23 concertos, traces inspirational sources. 417 musical examples. Second edition. 509pp.   21271-8 Paperbound $3.50

THE PERFECT WAGNERITE: A COMMENTARY ON THE NIBLUNG'S RING, George Bernard Shaw. Brilliant and still relevant criticism in remarkable essays on Wagner's Ring cycle, Shaw's ideas on political and social ideology behind the plots, role of Leitmotifs, vocal requisites, etc. Prefaces. xxi + 136pp.
(USO) 21707-8 Paperbound $1.50

DON GIOVANNI, W. A. Mozart. Complete libretto, modern English translation; biographies of composer and librettist; accounts of early performances and critical reaction. Lavishly illustrated. All the material you need to understand and appreciate this great work. Dover Opera Guide and Libretto Series; translated and introduced by Ellen Bleiler. 92 illustrations. 209pp.
21134-7 Paperbound $2.00

HIGH FIDELITY SYSTEMS: A LAYMAN'S GUIDE, Roy F. Allison. All the basic information you need for setting up your own audio system: high fidelity and stereo record players, tape records, F.M. Connections, adjusting tone arm, cartridge, checking needle alignment, positioning speakers, phasing speakers, adjusting hums, trouble-shooting, maintenance, and similar topics. Enlarged 1965 edition. More than 50 charts, diagrams, photos. iv + 91pp.   21514-8 Paperbound $1.25

REPRODUCTION OF SOUND, Edgar Villchur. Thorough coverage for laymen of high fidelity systems, reproducing systems in general, needles, amplifiers, preamps, loudspeakers, feedback, explaining physical background. "A rare talent for making technicalities vividly comprehensible," R. Darrell, *High Fidelity*. 69 figures. iv + 92pp.   21515-6 Paperbound $1.25

HEAR ME TALKIN' TO YA: THE STORY OF JAZZ AS TOLD BY THE MEN WHO MADE IT, Nat Shapiro and Nat Hentoff. Louis Armstrong, Fats Waller, Jo Jones, Clarence Williams, Billy Holiday, Duke Ellington, Jelly Roll Morton and dozens of other jazz greats tell how it was in Chicago's South Side, New Orleans, depression Harlem and the modern West Coast as jazz was born and grew. xvi + 429pp.
21726-4 Paperbound $2.50

FABLES OF AESOP, translated by Sir Roger L'Estrange. A reproduction of the very rare 1931 Paris edition; a selection of the most interesting fables, together with 50 imaginative drawings by Alexander Calder. v + 128pp. 6½x9¼.
21780-9 Paperbound $1.50

AGAINST THE GRAIN (A REBOURS), Joris K. Huysmans. Filled with weird images, evidences of a bizarre imagination, exotic experiments with hallucinatory drugs, rich tastes and smells and the diversions of its sybarite hero Duc Jean des Esseintes, this classic novel pushed 19th-century literary decadence to its limits. Full unabridged edition. Do not confuse this with abridged editions generally sold. Introduction by Havelock Ellis. xlix + 206pp.   22190-3 Paperbound $2.00

VARIORUM SHAKESPEARE: HAMLET. Edited by Horace H. Furness; a landmark of American scholarship. Exhaustive footnotes and appendices treat all doubtful words and phrases, as well as suggested critical emendations throughout the play's history. First volume contains editor's own text, collated with all Quartos and Folios. Second volume contains full first Quarto, translations of Shakespeare's sources (Belleforest, and Saxo Grammaticus), Der Bestrafte Brudermord, and many essays on critical and historical points of interest by major authorities of past and present. Includes details of staging and costuming over the years. By far the best edition available for serious students of Shakespeare. Total of xx + 905pp.
21004-9, 21005-7, 2 volumes, Paperbound $7.00

A LIFE OF WILLIAM SHAKESPEARE, Sir Sidney Lee. This is the standard life of Shakespeare, summarizing everything known about Shakespeare and his plays. Incredibly rich in material, broad in coverage, clear and judicious, it has served thousands as the best introduction to Shakespeare. 1931 edition. 9 plates. xxix + 792pp.   (USO) 21967-4 Paperbound $3.75

MASTERS OF THE DRAMA, John Gassner. Most comprehensive history of the drama in print, covering every tradition from Greeks to modern Europe and America, including India, Far East, etc. Covers more than 800 dramatists, 2000 plays, with biographical material, plot summaries, theatre history, criticism, etc. "Best of its kind in English," *New Republic*. 77 illustrations. xxii + 890pp.
20100-7 Clothbound $8.50

THE EVOLUTION OF THE ENGLISH LANGUAGE, George McKnight. The growth of English, from the 14th century to the present. Unusual, non-technical account presents basic information in very interesting form: sound shifts, change in grammar and syntax, vocabulary growth, similar topics. Abundantly illustrated with quotations. Formerly *Modern English in the Making*. xii + 590pp.
21932-1 Paperbound $3.50

AN ETYMOLOGICAL DICTIONARY OF MODERN ENGLISH, Ernest Weekley. Fullest, richest work of its sort, by foremost British lexicographer. Detailed word histories, including many colloquial and archaic words; extensive quotations. Do not confuse this with the Concise Etymological Dictionary, which is much abridged. Total of xxvii + 830pp. $6\frac{1}{2}$ x $9\frac{1}{4}$.
21873-2, 21874-0 Two volumes, Paperbound $6.00

FLATLAND: A ROMANCE OF MANY DIMENSIONS, E. A. Abbott. Classic of science-fiction explores ramifications of life in a two-dimensional world, and what happens when a three-dimensional being intrudes. Amusing reading, but also useful as introduction to thought about hyperspace. Introduction by Banesh Hoffmann. 16 illustrations. xx + 103pp.   20001-9 Paperbound $1.00

POEMS OF ANNE BRADSTREET, edited with an introduction by Robert Hutchinson. A new selection of poems by America's first poet and perhaps the first significant woman poet in the English language. 48 poems display her development in works of considerable variety—love poems, domestic poems, religious meditations, formal elegies, "quaternions," etc. Notes, bibliography. viii + 222pp.
22160-1 Paperbound $2.50

THREE GOTHIC NOVELS: THE CASTLE OF OTRANTO BY HORACE WALPOLE; VATHEK BY WILLIAM BECKFORD; THE VAMPYRE BY JOHN POLIDORI, WITH FRAGMENT OF A NOVEL BY LORD BYRON, edited by E. F. Bleiler. The first Gothic novel, by Walpole; the finest Oriental tale in English, by Beckford; powerful Romantic supernatural story in versions by Polidori and Byron. All extremely important in history of literature; all still exciting, packed with supernatural thrills, ghosts, haunted castles, magic, etc. xl + 291pp.
21232-7 Paperbound $2.50

THE BEST TALES OF HOFFMANN, E. T. A. Hoffmann. 10 of Hoffmann's most important stories, in modern re-editings of standard translations: Nutcracker and the King of Mice, Signor Formica, Automata, The Sandman, Rath Krespel, The Golden Flowerpot, Master Martin the Cooper, The Mines of Falun, The King's Betrothed, A New Year's Eve Adventure. 7 illustrations by Hoffmann. Edited by E. F. Bleiler. xxxix + 419pp.
21793-0 Paperbound $3.00

GHOST AND HORROR STORIES OF AMBROSE BIERCE, Ambrose Bierce. 23 strikingly modern stories of the horrors latent in the human mind: The Eyes of the Panther, The Damned Thing, An Occurrence at Owl Creek Bridge, An Inhabitant of Carcosa, etc., plus the dream-essay, Visions of the Night. Edited by E. F. Bleiler. xxii + 199pp.
20767-6 Paperbound $1.50

BEST GHOST STORIES OF J. S. LEFANU, J. Sheridan LeFanu. Finest stories by Victorian master often considered greatest supernatural writer of all. Carmilla, Green Tea, The Haunted Baronet, The Familiar, and 12 others. Most never before available in the U. S. A. Edited by E. F. Bleiler. 8 illustrations from Victorian publications. xvii + 467pp.
20415-4 Paperbound $3.00

MATHEMATICAL FOUNDATIONS OF INFORMATION THEORY, A. I. Khinchin. Comprehensive introduction to work of Shannon, McMillan, Feinstein and Khinchin, placing these investigations on a rigorous mathematical basis. Covers entropy concept in probability theory, uniqueness theorem, Shannon's inequality, ergodic sources, the E property, martingale concept, noise, Feinstein's fundamental lemma, Shanon's first and second theorems. Translated by R. A. Silverman and M. D. Friedman. iii + 120pp.
60434-9 Paperbound $1.75

SEVEN SCIENCE FICTION NOVELS, H. G. Wells. The standard collection of the great novels. Complete, unabridged. *First Men in the Moon, Island of Dr. Moreau, War of the Worlds, Food of the Gods, Invisible Man, Time Machine, In the Days of the Comet.* Not only science fiction fans, but every educated person owes it to himself to read these novels. 1015pp. (USO) 20264-X Clothbound $5.00

LAST AND FIRST MEN AND STAR MAKER, TWO SCIENCE FICTION NOVELS, Olaf Stapledon. Greatest future histories in science fiction. In the first, human intelligence is the "hero," through strange paths of evolution, interplanetary invasions, incredible technologies, near extinctions and reemergences. Star Maker describes the quest of a band of star rovers for intelligence itself, through time and space: weird inhuman civilizations, crustacean minds, symbiotic worlds, etc. Complete, unabridged. v + 438pp. (USO) 21962-3 Paperbound $2.50

THREE PROPHETIC NOVELS, H. G. WELLS. Stages of a consistently planned future for mankind. *When the Sleeper Wakes,* and *A Story of the Days to Come,* anticipate *Brave New World* and *1984,* in the 21st Century; *The Time Machine,* only complete version in print, shows farther future and the end of mankind. All show Wells's greatest gifts as storyteller and novelist. Edited by E. F. Bleiler. x + 335pp. (USO) 20605-X Paperbound $2.50

THE DEVIL'S DICTIONARY, Ambrose Bierce. America's own Oscar Wilde— Ambrose Bierce—offers his barbed iconoclastic wisdom in over 1,000 definitions hailed by H. L. Mencken as "some of the most gorgeous witticisms in the English language." 145pp. 20487-1 Paperbound $1.25

MAX AND MORITZ, Wilhelm Busch. Great children's classic, father of comic strip, of two bad boys, Max and Moritz. Also Ker and Plunk (Plisch und Plumm), Cat and Mouse, Deceitful Henry, Ice-Peter, The Boy and the Pipe, and five other pieces. Original German, with English translation. Edited by H. Arthur Klein; translations by various hands and H. Arthur Klein. vi + 216pp. 20181-3 Paperbound $2.00

PIGS IS PIGS AND OTHER FAVORITES, Ellis Parker Butler. The title story is one of the best humor short stories, as Mike Flannery obfuscates biology and English. Also included, That Pup of Murchison's, The Great American Pie Company, and Perkins of Portland. 14 illustrations. v + 109pp. 21532-6 Paperbound $1.25

THE PETERKIN PAPERS, Lucretia P. Hale. It takes genius to be as stupidly mad as the Peterkins, as they decide to become wise, celebrate the "Fourth," keep a cow, and otherwise strain the resources of the Lady from Philadelphia. Basic book of American humor. 153 illustrations. 219pp. 20794-3 Paperbound $1.50

PERRAULT'S FAIRY TALES, translated by A. E. Johnson and S. R. Littlewood, with 34 full-page illustrations by Gustave Doré. All the original Perrault stories— Cinderella, Sleeping Beauty, Bluebeard, Little Red Riding Hood, Puss in Boots, Tom Thumb, etc.—with their witty verse morals and the magnificent illustrations of Doré. One of the five or six great books of European fairy tales. viii + 117pp. 8⅛ x 11. 22311-6 Paperbound $2.00

OLD HUNGARIAN FAIRY TALES, Baroness Orczy. Favorites translated and adapted by author of the *Scarlet Pimpernel.* Eight fairy tales include "The Suitors of Princess Fire-Fly," "The Twin Hunchbacks," "Mr. Cuttlefish's Love Story," and "The Enchanted Cat." This little volume of magic and adventure will captivate children as it has for generations. 90 drawings by Montagu Barstow. 96pp. 22293-4 Paperbound $1.95

THE RED FAIRY BOOK, Andrew Lang. Lang's color fairy books have long been children's favorites. This volume includes Rapunzel, Jack and the Bean-stalk and 35 other stories, familiar and unfamiliar. 4 plates, 93 illustrations x + 367pp.
21673-X Paperbound $2.50

THE BLUE FAIRY BOOK, Andrew Lang. Lang's tales come from all countries and all times. Here are 37 tales from Grimm, the Arabian Nights, Greek Mythology, and other fascinating sources. 8 plates, 130 illustrations. xi + 390pp.
21437-0 Paperbound $2.50

HOUSEHOLD STORIES BY THE BROTHERS GRIMM. Classic English-language edition of the well-known tales — Rumpelstiltskin, Snow White, Hansel and Gretel, The Twelve Brothers, Faithful John, Rapunzel, Tom Thumb (52 stories in all). Translated into simple, straightforward English by Lucy Crane. Ornamented with head-pieces, vignettes, elaborate decorative initials and a dozen full-page illustrations by Walter Crane. x + 269pp.
21080-4 Paperbound $2.00

THE MERRY ADVENTURES OF ROBIN HOOD, Howard Pyle. The finest modern versions of the traditional ballads and tales about the great English outlaw. Howard Pyle's complete prose version, with every word, every illustration of the first edition. Do not confuse this facsimile of the original (1883) with modern editions that change text or illustrations. 23 plates plus many page decorations. xxii + 296pp.
22043-5 Paperbound $2.50

THE STORY OF KING ARTHUR AND HIS KNIGHTS, Howard Pyle. The finest children's version of the life of King Arthur; brilliantly retold by Pyle, with 48 of his most imaginative illustrations. xviii + 313pp. 6⅛ x 9¼.
21445-1 Paperbound $2.50

THE WONDERFUL WIZARD OF OZ, L. Frank Baum. America's finest children's book in facsimile of first edition with all Denslow illustrations in full color. The edition a child should have. Introduction by Martin Gardner. 23 color plates, scores of drawings. iv + 267pp.
20691-2 Paperbound $2.50

THE MARVELOUS LAND OF OZ, L. Frank Baum. The second Oz book, every bit as imaginative as the Wizard. The hero is a boy named Tip, but the Scarecrow and the Tin Woodman are back, as is the Oz magic. 16 color plates, 120 drawings by John R. Neill. 287pp.
20692-0 Paperbound $2.50

THE MAGICAL MONARCH OF MO, L. Frank Baum. Remarkable adventures in a land even stranger than Oz. The best of Baum's books not in the Oz series. 15 color plates and dozens of drawings by Frank Verbeck. xviii + 237pp.
21892-9 Paperbound $2.25

THE BAD CHILD'S BOOK OF BEASTS, MORE BEASTS FOR WORSE CHILDREN, A MORAL ALPHABET, Hilaire Belloc. Three complete humor classics in one volume. Be kind to the frog, and do not call him names . . . and 28 other whimsical animals. Familiar favorites and some not so well known. Illustrated by Basil Blackwell. 156pp.
(USO) 20749-8 Paperbound $1.50

EAST O' THE SUN AND WEST O' THE MOON, George W. Dasent. Considered the best of all translations of these Norwegian folk tales, this collection has been enjoyed by generations of children (and folklorists too). Includes True and Untrue, Why the Sea is Salt, East O' the Sun and West O' the Moon, Why the Bear is Stumpy-Tailed, Boots and the Troll, The Cock and the Hen, Rich Peter the Pedlar, and 52 more. The only edition with all 59 tales. 77 illustrations by Erik Werenskiold and Theodor Kittelsen. xv + 418pp. 22521-6 Paperbound $3.50

GOOPS AND HOW TO BE THEM, Gelett Burgess. Classic of tongue-in-cheek humor, masquerading as etiquette book. 87 verses, twice as many cartoons, show mischievous Goops as they demonstrate to children virtues of table manners, neatness, courtesy, etc. Favorite for generations. viii + 88pp. 6½ x 9¼. 22233-0 Paperbound $1.25

ALICE'S ADVENTURES UNDER GROUND, Lewis Carroll. The first version, quite different from the final *Alice in Wonderland,* printed out by Carroll himself with his own illustrations. Complete facsimile of the "million dollar" manuscript Carroll gave to Alice Liddell in 1864. Introduction by Martin Gardner. viii + 96pp. Title and dedication pages in color. 21482-6 Paperbound $1.25

THE BROWNIES, THEIR BOOK, Palmer Cox. Small as mice, cunning as foxes, exuberant and full of mischief, the Brownies go to the zoo, toy shop, seashore, circus, etc., in 24 verse adventures and 266 illustrations. Long a favorite, since their first appearance in St. Nicholas Magazine. xi + 144pp. 6⅝ x 9¼. 21265-3 Paperbound $1.75

SONGS OF CHILDHOOD, Walter De La Mare. Published (under the pseudonym Walter Ramal) when De La Mare was only 29, this charming collection has long been a favorite children's book. A facsimile of the first edition in paper, the 47 poems capture the simplicity of the nursery rhyme and the ballad, including such lyrics as I Met Eve, Tartary, The Silver Penny. vii + 106pp. (USO) 21972-0 Paperbound $1.25

THE COMPLETE NONSENSE OF EDWARD LEAR, Edward Lear. The finest 19th-century humorist-cartoonist in full: all nonsense limericks, zany alphabets, Owl and Pussycat, songs, nonsense botany, and more than 500 illustrations by Lear himself. Edited by Holbrook Jackson. xxix + 287pp. (USO) 20167-8 Paperbound $2.00

BILLY WHISKERS: THE AUTOBIOGRAPHY OF A GOAT, Frances Trego Montgomery. A favorite of children since the early 20th century, here are the escapades of that rambunctious, irresistible and mischievous goat—Billy Whiskers. Much in the spirit of *Peck's Bad Boy,* this is a book that children never tire of reading or hearing. All the original familiar illustrations by W. H. Fry are included: 6 color plates, 18 black and white drawings. 159pp. 22345-0 Paperbound $2.00

MOTHER GOOSE MELODIES. Faithful republication of the fabulously rare Munroe and Francis "copyright 1833" Boston edition—the most important Mother Goose collection, usually referred to as the "original." Familiar rhymes plus many rare ones, with wonderful old woodcut illustrations. Edited by E. F. Bleiler. 128pp. 4½ x 6⅜. 22577-1 Paperbound $1.00

Two Little Savages; Being the Adventures of Two Boys Who Lived as Indians and What They Learned, Ernest Thompson Seton. Great classic of nature and boyhood provides a vast range of woodlore in most palatable form, a genuinely entertaining story. Two farm boys build a teepee in woods and live in it for a month, working out Indian solutions to living problems, star lore, birds and animals, plants, etc. 293 illustrations. vii + 286pp.

20985-7 Paperbound $2.50

Peter Piper's Practical Principles of Plain & Perfect Pronunciation. Alliterative jingles and tongue-twisters of surprising charm, that made their first appearance in America about 1830. Republished in full with the spirited woodcut illustrations from this earliest American edition. 32pp. $4\frac{1}{2}$ x $6\frac{3}{8}$.

22560-7 Paperbound $1.00

Science Experiments and Amusements for Children, Charles Vivian. 73 easy experiments, requiring only materials found at home or easily available, such as candles, coins, steel wool, etc.; illustrate basic phenomena like vacuum, simple chemical reaction, etc. All safe. Modern, well-planned. Formerly *Science Games for Children*. 102 photos, numerous drawings. 96pp. $6\frac{1}{8}$ x $9\frac{1}{4}$.

21856-2 Paperbound $1.25

An Introduction to Chess Moves and Tactics Simply Explained, Leonard Barden. Informal intermediate introduction, quite strong in explaining reasons for moves. Covers basic material, tactics, important openings, traps, positional play in middle game, end game. Attempts to isolate patterns and recurrent configurations. Formerly *Chess*. 58 figures. 102pp. (USO) 21210-6 Paperbound $1.25

Lasker's Manual of Chess, Dr. Emanuel Lasker. Lasker was not only one of the five great World Champions, he was also one of the ablest expositors, theorists, and analysts. In many ways, his Manual, permeated with his philosophy of battle, filled with keen insights, is one of the greatest works ever written on chess. Filled with analyzed games by the great players. A single-volume library that will profit almost any chess player, beginner or master. 308 diagrams. xli x 349pp.

20640-8 Paperbound $2.75

The Master Book of Mathematical Recreations, Fred Schuh. In opinion of many the finest work ever prepared on mathematical puzzles, stunts, recreations; exhaustively thorough explanations of mathematics involved, analysis of effects, citation of puzzles and games. Mathematics involved is elementary. Translated by F. Göbel. 194 figures. xxiv + 430pp.

22134-2 Paperbound $3.00

Mathematics, Magic and Mystery, Martin Gardner. Puzzle editor for Scientific American explains mathematics behind various mystifying tricks: card tricks, stage "mind reading," coin and match tricks, counting out games, geometric dissections, etc. Probability sets, theory of numbers clearly explained. Also provides more than 400 tricks, guaranteed to work, that you can do. 135 illustrations. xii + 176pp.

20335-2 Paperbound $1.50

MATHEMATICAL PUZZLES FOR BEGINNERS AND ENTHUSIASTS, Geoffrey Mott-Smith. 189 puzzles from easy to difficult—involving arithmetic, logic, algebra, properties of digits, probability, etc.—for enjoyment and mental stimulus. Explanation of mathematical principles behind the puzzles. 135 illustrations. viii + 248pp.
20198-8 Paperbound $1.75

PAPER FOLDING FOR BEGINNERS, William D. Murray and Francis J. Rigney. Easiest book on the market, clearest instructions on making interesting, beautiful origami. Sail boats, cups, roosters, frogs that move legs, bonbon boxes, standing birds, etc. 40 projects; more than 275 diagrams and photographs. 94pp.
20713-7 Paperbound $1.00

TRICKS AND GAMES ON THE POOL TABLE, Fred Herrmann. 79 tricks and games—some solitaires, some for two or more players, some competitive games—to entertain you between formal games. Mystifying shots and throws, unusual caroms, tricks involving such props as cork, coins, a hat, etc. Formerly *Fun on the Pool Table.* 77 figures. 95pp.
21814-7 Paperbound $1.00

HAND SHADOWS TO BE THROWN UPON THE WALL: A SERIES OF NOVEL AND AMUSING FIGURES FORMED BY THE HAND, Henry Bursill. Delightful picturebook from great-grandfather's day shows how to make 18 different hand shadows: a bird that flies, duck that quacks, dog that wags his tail, camel, goose, deer, boy, turtle, etc. Only book of its sort. vi + 33pp. 6½ x 9¼.   21779-5 Paperbound $1.00

WHITTLING AND WOODCARVING, E. J. Tangerman. 18th printing of best book on market. "If you can cut a potato you can carve" toys and puzzles, chains, chessmen, caricatures, masks, frames, woodcut blocks, surface patterns, much more. Information on tools, woods, techniques. Also goes into serious wood sculpture from Middle Ages to present, East and West. 464 photos, figures. x + 293pp.
20965-2 Paperbound $2.00

HISTORY OF PHILOSOPHY, Julián Marías. Possibly the clearest, most easily followed, best planned, most useful one-volume history of philosophy on the market; neither skimpy nor overfull. Full details on system of every major philosopher and dozens of less important thinkers from pre-Socratics up to Existentialism and later. Strong on many European figures usually omitted. Has gone through dozens of editions in Europe. 1966 edition, translated by Stanley Appelbaum and Clarence Strowbridge. xviii + 505pp.   21739-6 Paperbound $3.50

YOGA: A SCIENTIFIC EVALUATION, Kovoor T. Behanan. Scientific but non-technical study of physiological results of yoga exercises; done under auspices of Yale U. Relations to Indian thought, to psychoanalysis, etc. 16 photos. xxiii + 270pp.
20505-3 Paperbound $2.50

Prices subject to change without notice.
Available at your book dealer or write for free catalogue to Dept. GI, Dover Publications, Inc., 180 Varick St., N. Y., N. Y. 10014. Dover publishes more than 150 books each year on science, elementary and advanced mathematics, biology, music, art, literary history, social sciences and other areas.